The NP Guide

Essential Knowledge for Nurse Practitioner Practice

4th Edition

Kevin L. Letz, DNP, MBA, RN, CNE, CEN, FNP-C, ANP-BC, PNP-BC, FAANP

Table of Contents

Preface

The healthcare field is undergoing drastic changes and whether we like it or not, business professionals are now driving how we as providers deliver healthcare services. We all know how important it is to maintain clinical skills and knowledge. I believe it is also now important to learn the business of being a clinician. I wrote this book because now is the time that every healthcare professional including nurse practitioners needs to have business savvy in addition to knowledge regarding patient care. I did not write this book to give you legal or accounting guidance. I am not a lawyer or an accountant. I consider myself an expert in health and wellness just like you and most practitioners and have developed knowledge in the business of medicine over time. I found it essential to know aspects of business practice to succeed in practice effectively. I am merely sharing some of my business knowledge with you so that you can practice effectively and succeed in your own career. Nurse practitioners have proven that they provide quality care in a cost--effective manner. I think what we have lacked as a profession is the business savvy to sell ourselves and effectively communicate our worth. In summation, clinicians who do not understand business principles as they relate to medical practice are in danger of becoming ineffective healers. This book provides the essential business knowledge nurse practitioners must have to respond to emerging challenges in a proactive way, rather than with fear and disappointment.

Dr. Kevin Letz

Chapter 1

The Role of the NP in the Current Health Care Environment

Many United States citizens and lawmakers contend that the U. S. health care system is in need of continued reform to increase access to healthcare and make healthcare more affordable. The U. S. spends far more per capita on health care than nearly all other industrialized nations and at the same time is looked upon as the best among the citizens of these same countries. However, discrepancies remain in cost per service and in standard patient outcome measures such as where the U. S. ranks in quality, access, and efficiency (The Common Wealth Fund, 2014). Improving the current health care system will take a commitment to a system that integrates clinical and financial information. In addition to the high cost of care provided in the U. S. other problems have been identified including poor accessibility to those with less financial means and a focus on illness and disease management rather than prevention and wellness services. To some degree, the shortage of primary care physicians in the 1960's brought about the role of the nurse practitioner (NP) and physician assistant (PA) to provide care to those having difficulty obtaining primary care services. Since that time, these non-physician clinicians have provided high quality services in a cost-effective manner. It is clear that, the expansion of the NP and PA professions can assist in correcting the majority of health care problems in the U. S. with the help of physicians and legislators. While improving, historically the cooperation of physicians and legislators to support non-physician providers has been lacking.

The Patient Protection and Affordable Care Act (ACA) (2010) passed in the United States Senate on December 24, 2009, and the US House of Representatives on March 21, 2010. President Obama signed it into law on March 23rd, 2010 and this was upheld by the Supreme Court on June 28, 2012. The ACA's main provisions provided for new benefits, rights and protections for US citizens, ensuring easier access to quality, affordable healthcare. Another goal of the ACA was to decrease the rate of growth of healthcare spending through health insurance reform, pushing for the main focus of healthcare on primary care versus secondary or tertiary care. This is already equating to an increased need of primary care providers in all areas of the United States (US Department of Human Services, 2013). Nurse practitioners will no doubt be an important part of the new health care system no matter how it is formulated, however, in what facet will have to be determined.

Healthcare consumers are much different than they were just 5 to 10 years ago. Consumers are now taking more control of their care and are demanding freedom of choice in providers even if they are given a list from which to choose. Health care consumers and the media are placing more emphasis on health promotion and illness prevention. However, the majority of consumers, lawmakers and the media are not informed that this is the primary scope of practice of the nurse practitioner. Nurse practitioners are trained not only to manage the common presenting illnesses and disease processes encountered in primary care but also in the art of providing patient education and counseling. Nurse practitioners also have the tremendous ability to build relationships with their patients, increasing both patient satisfaction and compliance and subsequently quality of care and better patient outcomes (Bauer, 2010).

Baby boomers and millennials are becoming older and requiring healthcare and at the same time the United States is beginning to experience the beginning of a primary care physician shortage. Many experts believe there will be a shortage of over 200,000 physicians in primary care by the year 2020. A vast majority of physicians provide care to patients in specialty practices, often times at a much higher rate of reimbursement the shortage of primary care physicians may break down barriers to practice for nurse practitioners. At the same time there exists a nursing shortage of over 200,000 that is expected to climb to 400,000 by the year 2020. NP's total over 130,000 and should reach numbers as high as 250,000 by 2020. The majority of nurse practitioners today practice in the traditional primary care specialties including family practice, pediatrics and ob-gyn practices. The increased complexity of patients and increasing number of specialty-trained physicians also creates the need for nurse practitioners in a variety of direct care roles in further specialized practices the market for NP's in acute care will increase as economists continue to keep a close eye on health care costs and funding of graduate medical education programs dries up.

Competition or Collaboration. Competition is important in any business, yet to improve access to care and cut spending then fair competition should be encouraged in the medical marketplace. Laws should guarantee a patient's right to choose among all qualified health professionals, not just HMO participating physicians. Congress and the White House should break up the medical monopoly that protects doctors from competition (which exists in nearly all other types of business) by other health professionals who are just as qualified meet the majority of our health care needs. Physicians should not have a monopoly on health care because they certainly do not have a monopoly on the knowledge of providing health care. Nurse practitioners can more than adequately provide the majority of duties involved in primary care and can be trained at 1/5th the cost.

The role of the physician will continue to play a vital role in the health of the US. Physicians will continually be needed to care for the truly ill patients who require more invasive testing and treatment modalities. Nurse practitioners will never threaten this role. Nurse practitioners will continue to fulfill the role of health maintenance, treatment of acute uncomplicated illness and the maintenance of chronic disease. This role is an area physicians are often choosing not to do. Complicated cases and conditions can easily be referred to a primary care physician or specialist in a similar way primary care physicians refer to specialists.

Critical Initiatives for NP's. There are three critical initiatives NP's must take while the health care system continues to undergo change. First, NPs must continue to provide patient and family centered primary care that focuses on disease prevention and health promotion. Providing high quality, cost conscious, patient centered care with a high level of patient satisfaction is what NP's do best and must continue to do so consistently. Colleges and universities that offer NP programs need to ensure that students graduate as competent, entry level NPs, prepared for the rigors of family practice.

Secondly, NPs must market their role. Expanding the knowledge of our role in health care to the public and other health care professionals is something NPs need to do consistently. NPs need to join their state and local NP groups and advocate for the profession. In the US the consumer will eventually have the largest say in the way the health care system evolves. Discussing the NP role with patients and other healthcare professionals will ultimately advance the profession the greatest.

Finally, fostering true collaboration with physician partners may be difficult since physicians have historically been practicing with limited competition. It is vital to educate physicians about how they can collaborate with NP's to provide higher quality care to more Americans.

References

Bauer, J. C. (2010). Nurse practitioners as an underutilized resource for health reform:

Evidence---based demonstration of cost---effectiveness. Journal of the American

Academy of Nurse Practitioners, 22(4), 228---231. doi: 10. 1111/j. 1745---

7599. 2010. 00498. x.

Patient Protection and Affordable Care Act, 42 U. S. C. § 18001 (2010). Retrieved from

http://housedocs. house. gov/energycommerce/ppacacon. pdf

The Common Wealth Fund (2014). Mirror, Mirror on the wall, 2014 update: how the

U. S. health care system compares internationally. Retrieved from

http://www. commonwealthfund. org/publications/fund---reports/2014/jun/mirror---

mirror

U. S. Department of Health and Human Services (2013). Creating jobs by addressing

primary care workforce needs. At HHS. gov/Health Care Retrieved from

http://www. hhs. gov/healthcare/facts/factsheets/2013/06/jobs06212012. html

Chapter 2

Certification and Licensure

NP education is not completed at graduation.

Regulation of a medical professional can be accomplished either through licensure or certification. Licensure is publicly controlled by the state or a governing authority which sets minimum standards for the profession in order for a person to practice under such title. The United States Constitution has delegated the states to oversee the professional licensure process and maintenance. State requirements vary, it is important to check the state's requirements before applying for an advanced practice license. The American Academy of Nurse Practitioners provides the following link on their website to assist nurse practitioners: https://www.aanp.org/legislation-regulation/state-legislation/state-practice-environment Chapter 3 discusses this topic in more detail.

Certification can be considered more of an option for the individual practitioner in that it is not necessary for practice in some states. Certification is often required for certain rights of practice such as prescriptive authority or government and third party payment. Some states require national certification as an advanced practice nurse as a prerequisite for APRN licensure. Certification always requires testing to establish certain high level knowledge in a particular field of study.

The American Nurses Credentialing Center (2016) defines certification as "the process by which a nongovernmental agency or an association grants recognition to an individual who has met certain predetermined qualifications. Certification can be used for entry into practice, validation of competence, recognition of excellence, and/or for regulation. It can be mandatory or voluntary. Certification validates an individual's knowledge and skills in a defined role and clinical area of practice, based on predetermined standards" (p.4).

Becoming Certified

Several organizations offer certification for advanced practice nurses (Table 2-1). Currently, states and organizations that require certification do not distinguish which organizations are preferred. The certifying organizations require master's degree or higher in nursing as part of eligibility to test. Each of the organizations has their own requirements in order to sit for their exams and this information can be obtained by contacting the organizations. Information regarding certification can be found on the organization's website.

All nurse practitioner certifying organizations require a master's degree or higher in nursing to meet eligibility to test. Each of the organizations has their own requirements in order to sit for their exams and this information can be obtained by contacting the organizations. Information regarding certification can be found on the organization's website. All certifying bodies have moved to computerized testing. The applicant must schedule a testing date after successful completion of the application. Benefits to computerized testing include the convenience of local testing sites, multiple testing dates per year and immediate preliminary results at the completion of the examination. Formal confirmation of examination results are sent within a few weeks of the test date.

Table 2-1	
Organizations Cost	Certification
AANP Cost: Member $240, Nonmember $315 www.aanp.org	Adult-Gerontology Primary Care Nurse Practitioner, Emergency Nurse Practitioner, Family Nurse Practitioner
ANCC Cost: ANA Member $270, Discount rate for AANP members $296 Nonmember $395 www.nursecredentialing.org	Adult-Gerontology Acute Care NP, Adult-Gerontology Primary Care NP, Family NP, Psychiatric-Mental Health NP, Pediatric Primary Care NP
National Certification Corporation for the Obstetrical, Gynecologic, and Neonatal NP Nursing Specialties exam cost: $ 325	Neonatal NP Women's Health NP

certificate maintenance: $100 www.nccwebsite.org	
Pediatric Nursing Certification Board Cost: $ 385 www.pncb.org	Pediatric NP

Preparing for Certification

You know better than anyone else your best method of preparation for an exam. The certification exams are no different. Several organizations are available to assist you in your studies with study books, tapes, and seminars. A search of the World Wide Web will provide you with many options for review materials.

Staying Certified

Each certification and each certification board has specific requirements for recertification. Check your certifying organization's website often for renewal information.

Hospital Privileges

Professional staff privileges often include the right to admit, treat, or consult on the clinical treatment of patients within the hospital setting. Less than 15% of nurse practitioners report having clinical staff privileges allowing them to admit and care for their own patients. While laws are usually quite lenient with regard to privileges for nurse practitioners and their practice in the hospital environment, hospitals often impose restrictions on privileges for non-physician providers. The Joint Commission on Accreditation of Healthcare Organizations (JCAHO) of which the majority of hospitals participate in does not require hospitals to grant privileges to nurse practitioner but does not disallow it. State laws vary but generally will allow privileges for nurse practitioners at some level. In most circumstances then it is up to the hospital whether they allow the granting of privileges to nurse practitioners. The Center for Medicare and Medicaid services actually recommends the diversification of hospital medical staff membership.

Obtaining hospital privileges is a process known as credentialing. The credentialing process usually begins by filling out an application for staff privileges and then later review by a medical staff board often consisting of physicians. Privileges are often determined by the state's Nurse Practice Act determination of advanced nursing scope of practice and the decisions of the hospitals credentialing committee. Generally speaking, there are two types of clinical privileges. Full privileges grant the practitioner to admit, write orders, and discharge etc. without supervision or co-signature of a physician. As noted, full privileges are rarely granted to nurse practitioners. Associate or extender privileges allow varying degrees of privileges but usually require direct oversight by a sponsoring physician. This form of privileges is what is most frequently given to the traditional rounding nurse or physician extender.

Having hospital privileges has its pros and cons that should be reviewed before deciding whether to take on this additional role. A few benefits of hospital privileges include heightening the visibility of nurse practitioners, maintaining continuity of care for your patients, and a chance to shift some responsibility off your collaborating physician and thus further increase your value to the practice. The drawbacks to having hospital privileges include the additional work, responsibility and risk that come along with such privileges. Rarely are nurse practitioners remunerated for the additional work involved with hospital care. Your decision on whether to obtain privileges should be based on the pros and cons above and your comfort level with hospital based care.

Professional Memberships

Belonging to a specialty organization has tremendous benefits including continuing education opportunities, networking, some degree of prestige, and a resource for further information. For most, it is not financially possible to join every nurse practitioner organization that exists, so some thought must go into your decision of which

organizations to join

.

American Association of Nurse Practitioners AANP National Administrative Office P.O. Box 12846 Austin, TX 78711 Phone: (512) 442-4262 Fax: (512) 442-6469 www.aanp.org

American College of Nurse Practitioner Faculty www.ACNPF.org

National Association of Pediatric Nurse Practitioners 5 Hanover Square Suite 1401 New York, NY 10004 Tel: 917-746-8300 Fax: 212-785-1713 www.napnap.org

American College of Nurse Midwives 8403 Colesville Rd, Suite 1550 Silver Spring, Maryland 20910 Phone: (240) 485-1800 Fax: (240) 485-1818 www.midwife.org

Association of Advanced Practice Psychiatric Nurses P.O. Box 7214 Tacoma, WA 98417-0214 Phone: (206) 524-4090 Fax: Fax: 253-590-0897 www.aappn.org

Alaska Nurse Practitioner Association 3701 E. Tudor Rd, Ste #208 Anchorage, AK 99507 Phone: (907) 222 6847 Fax: (907) 272 0292 www.anpa.enpnetwork.com

Arizona Nurse Practitioner Council Phoenix 1850 E. Southern Ave., Suite 1 Tempe, AZ 85282 Phone: (480) 831-0404 www.arizonanp.enpnetwork.com

Southern Arizona Nurse Practitioners 10981 N Black Canyon Ct. Oro Valley AZ 85737 (520) 544-9606 www.tucsonnp.com

Association of Women's Health, Obstetric, & Neonatal Nurses 2000 L Street, NW, Suite 740 Washington, D.C. 20036 Phone: (800) 673-8449 Fax: (202) 728-0575 www.awhonn.org

National Association of Neonatal Nurses 8735 W. Higgins Road, Suite 300 Chicago, IL 60631 Phone: 800.451.3795 http://www.nannp.org/

National Association of Nurse Practitioners in Women's Health 505 C Street, Northeast

Washington, D.C. 20002 Phone: (202) 543-9693 [SEP]www.npwh.org

Gerontological Advanced Practice Nurses Association (Formerly National Conference of Gerontological Nurse Practitioners) GAPNA National Office Box 56 East Holly Avenue, Pitman, NJ 08071-0056 Phone: (866) 355-1392 www.gapna.org

National Organization of Nurse Practitioner Faculties 1615 M Street, NW, Ste. 270 Washington, DC 20036 Tel: (202) 289-8044 Fax: (202) 289-8046 www.nonpf.com

California Coalition for Nurse Practitioners 1415 L Street, Suite 1000 Sacramento, CA 95814 Phone: (916) 441-1361 Fax: (916) 443-2004 www.canpweb.org

Connecticut Nurse Practitioner Group, Inc. 542 Hopmeadow Street PMB 143 Simsbury CT 06070-5405 www.nurse.org/ct/ cnpgi

Advanced Practice Nurse Council of the Delaware Nurses Association 4765 Ogletown Stanton Road, Suite L10 Newark, DE 19713 Phone: (302) 733-5880 www.denurses.org/apn_council

Nurse Practitioner Association of DC P0 Box 77424 Washington, DC 20013-7424 Phone: (202) 686-5514 www.npadc.org

Florida Association of Nurse Practitioners, Inc. PO Box 602 Lake Helen, FL 32744 Phone: 850.475.3280 http://www.flanp.org/

The United Advanced Practice Registered Nurses of Georgia 1035 Fielding Park Court Atlanta, GA 30319 Phone: (843) 732-0402 www.uaprn.org

Nurse Practitioner Council of Coastal GA PO Box 14046 [SEP]Savannah, Georgia 31416 Phone: (912) 351-7800 Fax: (912) 691-0229 npcouncilofcoastalga.enpnetwork.com

Hawaii Association of Professional Nurses P.O Box 4314 Honolulu, HI 96812 Tel: (808) 255C4442 Fax: (808) 593-7703 www. http://hapnurses.org/

Nurse Practitioner Conference Group of Idaho 967 E Parkcenter Blvd #225Boise, Idaho 83706 Phone: (208) 914-0138 www.npidaho.org

Illinois Society for Advanced Practice Nursing P.O. Box 636 Manteno, IL 60950 Phone:

815-468-8804 http://www.isapn.org/

Coalition of Advanced Practice Nurses of Indiana PO Box 87925 Canton, MI 48187 www.capni.org

Iowa Association of Nurse Practitioners https://iowaanp.enpnetwork.com/

Iowa Nurse Practitioner Society, Inc. 53 Norwood Circle Iowa City, IA 52245-5024 Phone: (319) 338-1051 www.iowanpsociety.org

Kansas Alliance of Advanced Nurse Practitioners PO Box 48423 Wichita, KS 67201 www.kaanpks.com

Kentucky Coalition of Nurse Practitioners and Nurse Midwives 1017 Ash Street Louisville, KY 40217 Phone: (502) 333-0076 www.kcnpnm.org

Louisiana Association of Nurse Practitioners 5713 Superior Drive, Suite A5 Baton Rouge, LA 70816 Phone (225) 293-7950 www.lanp.org

Maine Nurse Practitioner Association 11 Columbia Street Augusta, ME 04330 Phone: (207) 621-0313 Fax: (207) 622-4437 www.mnpa.us

Nurse Practitioner Association of Maryland PO Box 540 Ellicott City, MD 21041-0540 Phone: (888) 405-6726 Fax: (410) 772-7915 www.npamonline.org

Massachusetts Coalition of Nurse Practitioners P0 Box 1153 Littleton, MA 01460 Phone: (781) 575-1565 www.mcnpweb.org

Mississippi Association of Nurse Practitioners 152 Watford Parkway Drive Ste 109 Canton, Mississippi 39046 Phone: 601.407.3226 Fax: 601.510.7833 http://www.msanp.org/

Missouri Nurses Association 1904 Bubba Lane PO Box 105228 Jefferson City, MO 65110 Phone: (573) 636-4623 Fax: (573) 636-9576 www.missourinurses.org

Advanced Practice Nurses of the Ozarks PO Box 14308 Springfield MO 65814 http://www.apno.net/

Nevada Nurses Association PO Box 34660 Reno, NV 89533 Phone: (775) 747-2333 www.nvnurses.org

Nevada Advanced Practice Nurses Association (NAPNA) P.O. Box 50541 Sparks, Nevada 89435 http://www.napna.net

New Hampshire NP Association 180 Mutton Road, Webster, NH 03303 Phone: (603) 648-2233 Fax: (603) 648-2466 www.npweb.org

New Jersey State Nurses Association 1479 Pennington Road Trenton, NJ 08618 Phone: (609) 883-5335 Fax: (609) 883-8343 www.njsna.org

New Mexico Nurse Practitioner Council PO Box 40682 Albuquerque, NM 87196C0682 Phone: (505) 366-3763 www.nmnpc.org

Nurse Practitioner Association New York State (The NPA) 12 Corporate Drive Clifton Park, NY 12065 Phone: (518) 348-0719 Fax: (518) 348-0720 https://www.thenpa.org/

North Carolina Nurses Association Council of NPs 103 Enterprise St. Raleigh, NC 27607 Phone: (919) 821C4250 Fax: (919) 829-5807 www.ncnurses.org

Association of Oklahoma Nurse Practitioners 100 Park Ave, Ste. 710 Oklahoma City OK 73102 Telephone: (405) 445-4874 Fax: (405) 445-4864 http://www.npofoklahoma.com

Nurse Practitioners of Oregon 18765 SW Boones, Ferry Road Suite 200, Tualatin, OR 97062 Phone: (503) 293-0011 www.nursepractitionersoforegon.org

Pennsylvania Coalition of Nurse Practitioners PO Box 1071 Jenkintown, PA 19046 Phone: (866) 800-6206 Fax: (866) 217-1751 SEP www.pacnp.org

Pennsylvania Coalition of Nurse Practitioners 2400 Ardmore Blvd: Suite 302: Pittsburgh, PA 15221 Phone: 412.243.6149 fax: 412.243.5160 pcnp@pacnp.org

Advanced Practice Registered Nurse Council of the South Carolina Nurses Association 1821 Gadsden Columbia, SC 29201 Phone: (803) 252C4781 Fax: (803) 779-3870 www.scnurses.org

Upstate Nurse Practitioner Association (SC) http://upstatenursepractitioner.com/

Low Country Advanced Nurse Practitioners Association http://lcapn.org/index.php

Nurse Practitioner Association of South Dakota PO Box 2822 SEP Rapid City, SD 57709
www.npasd.org

Tennessee Nurses Association Council of Advanced Practice Nurses 545 Mainstream
Drive, Suite 405 Nashville, TN 37228-1296 Phone: (615) 254-0350 www.tnaonline.org

Texas Nurse Practitioners 4425 S. Mopac Expressway Building III, Suite 405 Austin, TX
78735 Phone: (512) 291-6224 Fax: (512) 291-6225 www.texasnp.org

Vermont Nurse Practitioners Association PO Box 64773 Burlington, VT 05406
www.vtnpa.enpnetwork.com

Virginia Council of Nurse Practitioners 250 West Main Street, Suite 100 Charlottesville, VA
22902 Phone: (434) 977-3716 Fax: (434) 979-2439 www.vcnp.net

ARNPs United of Washington State 10024 SE 240th Street, Suite 230 Kent, WA 98031
Phone: (253) 480C1035 Fax: (253) 852-7725 www.auws.org

Metro Milwaukee Nurse Practitioners PO Box 13674 Wauwatosa, WI 53213-0674 Phone:
(414) 297-9416 www.metromilwaukeenp.enpnetwork.com

References

American Nurses Credentialing Center (2016). *Certification: General testing and renewal*

handbook. MD: ANCC. www.nursecredentialing.org

Chapter 3

Prescriptive and Legal Authority for Nurse Practitioners

Always ask yourself "Is there any reason why the patient shouldn't receive this drug?"

Prescriptive authority for nurse practitioners has been a key factor in the credibility and expansion of the nurse practitioner role. Without prescriptive authority it would be difficult for nurse practitioners to become primary care providers or to function in any independent role. The expansion of prescriptive authority has and will likely continue to be met with resistance. While physicians focus much of their attention on the expansion of nurse practitioner roles, other professions including pharmacists, optometrists, and psychologists, are looking for ways to gain or expand prescriptive authority.

Every state addresses prescriptive authority for nurse practitioners. The following is a summary of prescriptive authority among all states. Individual state regulations may change and it is important to check with your state board of nursing for current rules and regulations. Contact your state board of nursing for requirements in obtaining prescriptive authority. The Drug Enforcement Agency (DEA) has application forms online for NPs to apply for DEA numbers for those who live in states where this is granted (https://www. deadiversion. usdoj. gov/webforms/).

States where NPs may prescribe with physician involvement or delegation of prescriptive writing by a physician. NPs may not prescribe controlled substances in these states.

Florida (NPs may prescribe controlled substances in Florida beginning 01/01/2017).

States were NPs may prescribe with physician involvement or delegation of prescription writing by a physician. NPs may prescribe controlled substances in these states.

Alabama, Arkansas, California, Delaware, Illinois, Indiana, Kansas, Kentucky, Louisiana, Massachusetts, Michigan, Mississippi, North Carolina, New Jersey, Louisiana, Mississippi, New York, Ohio, Oklahoma, Pennsylvania, South Carolina, South Dakota, Tennessee, Utah, Virginia, Vermont, West Virginia, Wisconsin.

States were NPs may prescribe independently of a physician. Controlled Substances may be prescribed as well

Alaska, Arizona, Colorado, Connecticut, District of Columbia, Hawaii, Idaho, Iowa, Maine, Maryland, Minnesota, Montana, Nebraska, Nevada, New Hampshire, New Mexico, North Dakota, Oregon, Rhode Island, Vermont, Washington, Wyoming.

Scope of Practice for Nurse Practitioners

The American Association of Nurse Practitioners (AANP) divides the country into three distinct practice environments for nurse practitioners. The environments range from least restrictive to most restrictive. The AANP defines and categorizes the states into full practice, reduced practice, and restricted practice.

Full Practice: State practice and licensure law provides for nurse practitioners to evaluate patients, diagnose, order and interpret diagnostic tests, and initiate and manage treatments. This includes prescribing medications under the exclusive licensure authority of the state board of nursing. This is the model recommended by the Institute of Medicine and National Council of State Boards of Nursing.

Alaska, Arizona, Colorado, Connecticut, District of Columbia, Hawaii, Idaho, Iowa, Maine, Maryland, Minnesota, Montana, Nebraska, Nevada, New Hampshire, New Mexico, North Dakota, South Dakota, Oregon, Rhode Island, Vermont, Washington, Wyoming.

Reduced Practice: State practice and licensure law reduces the ability of nurse practitioners to practice. State requires a formal collaborative agreement with an outside health discipline in order for the NP to provide patient care.

Alabama, Arkansas, Delaware, Illinois, Indiana, Kansas, Kentucky, Louisiana, Mississippi, New Jersey, New York, Ohio, Pennsylvania, South Dakota, Utah, West Virginia, Wisconsin.

Restricted Practice: State practice and licensure law restricts the ability of a nurse practitioner to practice. State requires supervision, delegation, or team management by an outside health discipline in order for the NP to provide patient care.

California, Florida, Georgia, Massachusetts, Michigan, Missouri, North Carolina, Oklahoma, South Carolina, Tennessee, Texas, Virginia.

The legal authority for nurse practitioners varies widely across the United States. As barriers for NPs continue to fall, more states will move toward the full practice model. Nurse practitioners can facilitate this move by being politically active and aware of the issues that impact their practice.

References

American Association of Nurse Practitioners. (AANP) (2013) Nurse Practitioner State

Practice Environment, retrieved from www.APRN.Org

Chapter 4

Searching, Landing, and Starting a New Position

"Never talk negatively about present or previous employers during an interview"

Employment Options for NP's

Clinicians entering practice today are confronted with a more complicated and diverse business environment than in years' past. This increase in business complexity, resulting from the rapid restructuring of the National health care delivery system opens up new, diverse opportunities to clinicians. Understanding key organizational models available to clinicians is critical. Each option has strengths and weaknesses that you must weigh in order to evaluate which environment is best for you.

Hospital Practice

Hospitals can employ NPs for both inpatient and outpatient services. Inpatient NP services are typically billed under Medicare Part B Guidelines (CMS, 2014). If an NP is a hospital employee, the NP services are often bundled under the daily bed rate and not independently under the provider. In this instance hospital billing teams code the charts and services accordingly.

If the NP is an employee of an outside practice or organization while providing services inpatient, then the independent and "incident to" billing requirements would be followed according to CMS guidelines (CMS, 2014). The NP may be required to track and submit their own billing. It is important to have a clear understanding of the "incident-to" billing guidelines for inpatient services as they can be difficult to follow correctly. Additionally, it is important to be sure a physician is not billing for the same services as the NP on the same date.

Nursing Home Practice

Many NP's find nursing homes and assisted living facilities to be a great fit for their skills and services. In most cases providers can see patients at their own speed and are not pushed to meet a daily quota of visits. Patients in these facilities also often lack the preventative care NPs provide. The care of residents in skilled facilities must be under the supervision of a physician who is available by phone in an emergency according to federal law at the time of publication (CMS, 2014). The federal law also stipulates that at the option of a state, the NP can provide the care if done in collaboration with a physician and not employed by the facility.

Group Practice Without Walls (GPWW)

A model often described as a group practice without walls has emerged as a hybrid between solo and group practice. Members of the practice agree to maintain independent offices yet agree to share key components of the office practice such as billing, management of accounts receivable, and other key fiscal operations.   Potential for conflict may exist with less control over daily business functions. The model may exist in different legal forms, to include partnerships, limited liability companies, and professional corporations.

Single Specialty Group Practice

Single specialty group practice is the combination of two or more specialists in the same field to create a group. The benefits of a specialty group practice in addition to the sharing of key office functions as outlined with GPWW include sharing of office space and call coverage. These groups have been very popular in the last several years and many are run by physician practice management companies that can leverage lucrative contracts.

Multi---Specialty Group Practice

A trend in many larger markets has been the consolidation of groups to form large multi---specialty groups. The development of such groups has been driven by the need for greater efficiency, the impact of competitive markets, the effect of large managed care contracts, and the relative stability offered by a larger organization. The majority of multi---specialty groups would be organized as corporations, partnerships or foundations.

Independent Practice

Independent practice is traditionally the first choice among physicians but rare for the practicing NP. A solo practice involves operating independently and managing the day to day operations independent of other providers. Most states require collaboration with a physician for chart review and prescriptive privileges. Hospital privileges and on call coverage may be barriers to independent practice unless the NP has an agreement with a physician.

Evaluating the Right Practice Model for You- Know Your Self First

It's important to have a clear understanding of what you envision for your career before evaluating practice models. Do you have family obligations that require you to be home by a certain time every day? Do you want to work weekends? Do you want to be on call? Do you want to work a flexible shift/ location or do you want the ability to blend inpatient/outpatient time with time working from home? Are you the sole household income and therefore need job stability and full benefits? Or is you job the secondary income that can allow for some flexibility in hours and pay? The choice you make will also depend on the level of autonomy you would like to have balanced with the level of risk and stability. Doing an honest evaluation of what your ideal job looks like will help prevent accepting a job you are unhappy with. The next step is to perform an in-depth evaluation of the practice models in the job areas that interest you. Major processes of the decision- making process may include talking with colleagues, seeking counsel from an accountant and attorney, and completing a personal inventory or your interests and needs.

Searching

Searching for a nurse practitioner position should not be done in the same manner as looking for a nursing position. You will not find thousands of ads by opening your newspaper, all of them specific to your specialty and location you want to practice. Searching for a nurse practitioner position becomes much more difficult and often times you will have to create one. There are several steps involved in searching for a nurse practitioner position that may make the process a little easier.

Step One: Choose a Geographic Location

The first step in searching for a position is to determine where you are willing to live. There is no sense in searching for a position throughout the country if you have no plans of moving out of the town you currently live in (even if there are no jobs).

Step Two: Choose Your Specialty

The second step in searching is to decide what type of practice setting you hope to work in and the type of specialty you wish to practice. You may think because you are trained in pediatrics for example that you have no choice but to practice in a pediatrician's office or pediatric floor. In reality, there are many more options. Maybe you have a special interest in diabetes care and thus could consider approaching a pediatric endocrinologist in town. Just as well you could approach that large pediatrics group in town and sell the idea of doing the routine follow up

care for all the diabetic children in the practice.

Understand that your specialty choice also drives salary ranges. Be realistic

about the pay scale in your specialty area. Documents such as the Nurse

Practitioner Perspective and Advance Healthcare Network for NPs & PAs Annual

Salary Survey (Hopf, 2014) are a great resource for understanding Salary

expectations based on geographic location as well as specialty.

Step Three: Look for What Is Available

Checking the classified ads has become such an easy task with the world---wide---

web. Multiple sites are available that are specific to health care or even nurse

practitioners (www. aanp. org, www. nursecredentialing. org) in addition to sites that

cover multiple careers (www. indeed. com). Networking with faculty and peers on

social media sites such as Linked In has become an increasing source of job

opportunities. Building relationships with other healthcare providers is essential to

researching job opportunities. If you are interested in a particular hospital or

organization search their 'careers' tab on their websites for open positions.

Step Four: Creating a Position

Often times your best bet is creating a position. This is especially true if you find

nothing advertised that fits your niche. This is not at hard as it sounds but requires

the ability to sell both yourself and the NP profession. Send out information packets to potential practices as well as approaching colleagues in your network to inquire about creating a new position. Often times you can identify a need for an NP role during a clinical rotation while working as a staff nurse during school. Information packets can include your curriculum vitae (CV) and cover letter along with information about NPs. A nurse practitioner fact sheet that references studies documenting nurse practitioner quality care and high patient satisfaction may be appropriate. Many of the NP organizations described previously have developed brochures or flyers that can be used. Focus attention on practices that fit your interest and who you know are "busting at the seams" busy. A busy practice may feel the need for another provider but not have the time to look for help. A week or so after you have sent the packet then go visit the medical director to introduce yourself and the benefits of nurse practitioners to a practice and to them in particular. Be ready to discuss the financial aspect of incorporating your role into their practice including costs and revenue. It may help to know their least favorite thing to do in practice (whether it be pelvic exams, taking call, or administrative duties) and offer your expertise in this area.

The Application Process

The application process is often initiated by either sending a cover letter/ CV in response to an advertisement or filling out an online application. Just as a builder needs a hammer and nails to construct a building to sell, you need a CV and cover letter to sell yourself. These documents can also be electronically incorporated into an online application to highlight your skill set and experience.

The Cover Letter

The cover letter must be of such high quality that the job searcher will both look at your attached CV and call you for an interview. The sole purpose of the cover letter is to get your foot in the door with an interview. The cover letter should be brief (less than 1 page) and professionally written. Careful attention to grammar indicates you are a thorough and detailed-oriented person. The letter should introduce you and your best qualities and relay your interest in the advertised position. The letter should not go into detail but just arouse enough interest in the reader to look at your attached CV. A well- written cover letter should allow you to do three things:

Relay the Reason for Your Interest

Personalize and target yourself to the particular organization that you are applying to. Don't try to make one cover letter fit all situations. Take the time to modify it to the situation.

Market a specific subset of skills that you have. If you are a novice NP then mention the experience you have had as a registered nurse.

There are a few "essentials" of a cover letter (Innes, 2012). Essential items to include are your contact information, the date, the address of the advertiser, and where you heard of the position being sought. The cover letter should be on good quality bond paper and have a clean, crisp look. There is no reason to add fancy designs, covers or folders. Don't forget to sign the letter and triple check the spelling and grammar for errors. Remember a cover letter alone will not get you a position but will likely be the first thing the employer sees, so make it a good impression.

Resume / Curriculum Vitae

A resume and curriculum vitae (CV) both serve as detailed outlines of your professional experience, training, and credentials. The main difference between a resume and CV are their length. A CV goes into greater depth with regard to publications, conference attendance, and academic achievements. The main components of both include your contact (including all phone numbers, email address, postal address) your educational background, previous employment, awards and certifications, memberships, community service. A resume or CV is often used as a screening device by the employer to determine whom they should interview. Employers usually have an idea of the type of person they are looking for, hoping to find people with a certain educational background or skill set. Write your resume or CV with this in mind, as just like the cover letter, the goal is to get you an interview. The resume should show that some research has been done to match your skills and with the employer's needs. Successful job hunters convince employers they will become an asset to them. With the advent of online applications, you may find the

CV does not come into play until you are actually in a face to face interview. It is appropriate to bring a copy of your CV to a face to face interview for the employer to refer to and share with colleagues involved in the hiring process.

There are two main types of resumes often labeled chronological and functional. The chronological resume is the most traditional format, which chronologically lists your experiences etc. starting with the most recent. The chronological approach is good for those whose career or educational path have experienced constant growth or for those who have work in progress. The chronological approach is not the best choice for those who have gaps in their career or for those with limited experience. A functional resume emphasizes special skills and accomplishments in order of significance to the position you are applying for. A functional resume stresses what it is you do, rather than what you have done. This type of resume is best for those with limited experiences or training and is not recommended for more professional roles such as NP's. There is no law against combining these two formats as well highlighting both your training and experiences in addition to your specific skill sets, which would be missed in the chronological resume.

The resume should be:

---Pleasing to the eye

---Honest

---Printed on one side of 8½ x 11 sheet of high quality paper- if presented in a face to face interview

---Neatly typed on clean neutral color paper with black ink

The resume should <u>not</u>:

---Be without a cover letter

---Have misspelled words

---Include salary needs

---Include reasons for leaving a position

---Start with the word "Resume"

Professional Portfolio

A professional portfolio is a collection of awards, published papers, and projects for the employer to visualize. It should also include any volunteer activities that involve healthcare such as sports physical clinics, blood pressure screenings or lecturing at elementary schools on health and safety.

It often goes beyond traditional work experience and includes other meaningful activities that highlight your skills and enthusiasm about your role. Many nursing experts recommend using a portfolio, however it's important to focus on what each individual employer is looking for in a potential employee. Is this a community based position focusing on the underserved? Then by all means, highlight your charity work and volunteer efforts. Is this a fast-Paced Intensive care unit? Then your critical care certification and experience in Advanced Cardiac Life Support should be front and center in the portfolio.

The First

Interview

After you have submitted your CV and have had an initial telephone interview or discussion, you are ready for your first face-face interview. This initial meeting serves mostly as a "get to know" each other meeting. Both you and the interviewer will likely seek to impress one another. Allow the interviewer to lead the conversation, allowing them to talk either about themselves or the practice. Listen attentively as the information they give you will provide you useful information as the interview continues and will tell you a lot about their overall philosophy of the practice. If the interviewer does not openly talk about themselves or the practice then ask questions of them along this level. Most people enjoy discussing themselves or their organization if they are proud of it. Ask about their philosophy or style of practicing medicine or the goals of the organization. You are certain to have more questions about how the practice will benefit you (such as how much money you will be making) but hold these back for the second interview. Be attentive as to how your interviewer is presenting themselves as well. Do they make direct eye contact with you? Do they switch subjects or not answer the questions you ask them? Does the interviewer interrupt you when you are talking or do they appear as if they are waiting for you to stop talking, which may be a sign that they do not respect you as a peer. Skilled interviewers and employers know that while medical knowledge can be trained and learned, personality and attitude are generally ingrained traits in a potential employee. They are looking to see if you are engaging, kind, attentive and pick up on social cues and clues.

When the interviewer does ask you questions then take a few seconds to collect your thoughts instead of rushing to answer the question. Answer questions succinctly and using proper English. Feel free to include important buzz words such as 'clinical expertise', 'patient satisfaction', and 'revenue stream' to demonstrate your knowledge of the important components of healthcare delivery

Make sure you think about why they are asking the question before you answer. Avoid making negative comments or remarks about previous employers or health care situations. If the interview makes such comments and you want to agree that is fine but do not initiate negative discussions. Be sure to know your answers to the most common questions asked in a first interview such as: 1) What are your goals for the next   # of years?, 2) What is your best quality?, 3) What is your worst quality?, 4) What can you bring to this setting? These answers show your own self-awareness. Indicating that you have no "worst qualities" or no "areas of weakness" implies a lack of insight into your skills. Turn that negative into a positive by indicating intent to improve upon any weakness. The key to the first interview is to leave a positive impression and to present a win-win situation. Key outcomes your employer can expect are a lightened load from your hiring both clinically and administratively and increased revenue for the practice. Be able to provide a specific example of how your salary will be supported by patient load and revenue from your practice.

Make sure that the interviewer knows that you are interested in the position and excited about the opportunity. Always follow up after the first interview. Send a thank you letter via postal mail the same day of the interview and again let them know that you are interested. Clarify the follow up communication. Will the interview call you whether you've been selected or not? When will they be making their decision? Can you follow a provider in the clinic in the meantime?

Key Interviewing Strategies

Show respect to the interviewer.

Listen attentively when the interviewer is talking and answer questions honestly.

Put your phone away. Put your phone away! Put your phone away. . . . . Did I say put your phone away? Put your phone on vibrate or silence. You should be actively engaged in the interview and focused only on this process.

Be open about your past.

Be ready to discuss employment gaps and previous positions that did not work out in a convincing yet honest manner.

Keep the conversation positive at all costs.

Be confident yet humble.

Do your homework.

Be familiar with both the practice and the specialty in which
you are interviewing. Knowledge is power.

Show your flexibility. As nurses we all have multiple talents. Be sure the
interviewer is aware that you can and are willing to do more than just perform
direct patient care.

Learn about the interviewer. Don't be afraid to ask questions of the interviewer
but try asking questions that interest them. Understanding the person interviewing
you will give you a greater chance of having a conversation that leads to highlighting
how you can help them.

Money talks, Last. It is not wrong to discuss money during the interview
but do not negotiate actual numbers until later interviews. It is generally
advised to discuss salary last or to even wait until a second or third
interview. It is always advisable to wait for the employer to identify the salary
range first.

"Dress and attitude" Lastly, don't forget the essentials of a good
interview including conservative business attire, a positive attitude, and a

professional, confident demeanor. Arriving for an NP job interview in scrubs or other hospital attire is not acceptable. You are transitioning to a professional role and professional attire does not include scrubs, denim, yoga pants or other athleisure wear (Reeves, 2009).

The Second Interview

Before going to the second interview you should plan on doing a little background check on your potential new employer. Find out what you can about the supervising physician's reputation and track record. A small amount of time now can save you from some unpleasant revelations later. Check with your state's medical regulatory board for pending or previous malpractice suits or license suspensions. A few lawsuits are not atypical but if there are a number of suits filed against the same practitioner this may be a red flag. Malpractice insurers are required to report payments made for malpractice claims to the National Practitioner Data Bank.

The second interview will likely be much longer and more in-depth. You should ask to follow the supervising physician and any other NP employees during their day. Observing how the practitioner and office functions can give you a lot of information that would not come about in discussion. This also helps you see the philosophy of the organization. Are they judicious with antibiotic and narcotic prescriptions or do they put pleasing the patient first over guidelines? The layout of an office can be quite important as well. If the plan is for you to function with the use of just one exam room it may be difficult for you to see enough patients and thus be profitable. If space is limited then find out how the practice may expand for future growth. The second interview should serve to function as finding out more about the practice, how it functions, and how you will work within the practice. Of course, you will also want to find out more about benefits, hours, and further expectations such as being on call or performing hospital rounds during the second interview.

The interviewer will want to know more about your practice style and how well you will fit into their practice model. Be ready to sell yourself and your profession. Even as a new nurse practitioner you likely have a wealth of experience and expertise as an RN so do not sell yourself short. Emphasize your educational preparation along with your previous experiences in health care even if it is not as an NP. Discuss the health maintenance and prevention approach of nurse practitioners in addition to our diagnosis and treatment ability. Be sure to bring up special interests or skills you bring to the table such as experience performing pap smears or your suturing ability.

Again, do not forget to ask for the job you are interviewing for. You must make sure that the interviewer knows that you are interested in the position and excited at the opportunity. An additional meeting may be appropriate in a more social setting such as over dinner or at one of your homes with your families. How the spouses interrelate with each other is more important than you may think. A working relationship does not require a close social friendship but a nonprofessional level of communication is very helpful. If you are not married then you may not be comfortable with meeting your potential employer alone in this type of social setting. Invite a mutual friend or ask for the practice manager or another important team member of the practice to attend. Keep alcohol intake to a minimum at these events.

Observation Period

Scheduling additional time with one of the practitioners in observation can be very helpful in deciding whether you and the practice are a good fit. If you are not yet out of your training program try to schedule clinical time with the nurse practitioners or physicians in the practice. If you are already out of school then volunteer to spend some unpaid observation time at the practice. Spend as much time possible with the supervising physician. Determining his/her clinical preferences will improve collaboration in the future. The extra time will also give you an opportunity to understand the ground rules when you are working more independently. During this observation period you can learn a lot by asking questions of the nurses and office staff and achieve a sense of whether they are happy with what they are doing and how they are treated by the management team. You can also get a feeling of how receptive the office staff is of having a nurse practitioner provider onboard. Leaving a positive impression with the other staff can lean in your favor because they will often give the interviewer their impression of you. Be willing to share personal information as long as you do not think it will hinder you and learn as much personal information of other staff members to achieve a good working relationship before you are even hired.

Evaluating an Offer

A job offer from a private or group practice is very different from that of a hospital as is a nurse practitioner offer is from a registered nursing position. You have more leverage to negotiate salary and benefits because you are now in a role that generates revenue. Evaluating an offer requires rating the pros and cons of the offer as well as comparing the offer to your list of needs. Be ready with a list of compromises you are willing to make. For example, if the practice does not cover the cost of lab coats. Be prepared to supply your own lab coat. Be reasonable in what you will accept and what you will walk away for. Walking away from an otherwise idea job because they do not provide lab coats makes you appear inflexible and unreasonable. Reasons to turn down a job include excessive expectations of workload, unsafe of illegal practices, or a schedule that doesn't suit your home life. If you are going to negotiate the starting salary offer, be prepared to provide data to support your stance on salary request. Make sure you are aware of what similar roles in the community include regarding salary and benefits packages.

Evaluating an Opportunity

☐ How many patient rooms will you be working out of?

☐ Is there space for future growth?

☐ Are there enough support staff to handle your arrival?

☐ Is there a lot of staff turnover?

☐ What is the office overhead?

☐ Is there space in the office for your office / consultation room?

☐ How will the practice promote your arrival?

☐ How many patients do they see and do they plan for you to see?

☐ How is the on-call coverage handled?

☐ How is provider time off handled in the practice?

☐ Will you have access to the practice's profit and loss statements and other

financial records to track your productivity?

☐ Is there an orientation period?

☐ How long does it take for a new patient to schedule an appointment?

☐ How long does a patient usually wait to be seen by the provider?

☐ What is the ratio of nurse / provider?

☐ Is the office space owned or leased and for what period?

☐ Are there other duties you will be expected to do besides patient care management such as bring back your own patients?

 Can you pursue other opportunities such as research studies?

 Is there equipment to perform procedures (rigid sigmoid etc.)?

 Do the employees appear happy and satisfied?

 Does the supervising physician have time for you to ask questions through the day?

If you find that you and the practice or physician(s) are not a good fit then do not waste each other's time. Write a letter thanking the interviewer for their time and opportunity and then gracefully state that you are not interested in the position. Don't go into detail as to why but rather just mention that it is not a good fit. You will likely meet up with this person again and you do not want to create an uncomfortable situation or relationship.

Making the step toward commitment

If you are offered the position verbally and are definitely interested then accept the position. The details can be worked out later and you will not be bound to a verbal acceptance. A written document will supersede the oral agreement. Write up a letter of intent or have your lawyer do it. A letter of intent can put in writing your requirements for the position or may just put in writing the areas you have already discussed. If the employer finds this acceptable then an employment contract can be drawn up. Read your employment contract or employee manual thoroughly to save yourself from surprises down the road. Most experts even recommend having a lawyer read it over which can save you some time and also allow for some clarification. Do not begin working until a written contract is in place.

Starting Out

Schedule extra time outside of your assigned working hours to refine your clinical skills and to become familiar with the culture and staff of the organization. Making a good impression and doing a good job for the patient and your employer take much more time than you ever would have imagined when you were in school. Learning doesn't end when you graduate from NP school and, in fact, you may find yourself reviewing more pathophysiology and disease-related content now then you did while in school. Take time to review any cases which contained unfamiliar disease processes or required you to perform a new skill. Review the guidelines for the diagnoses and treatment of that disease or review a textbook on how to effectively perform the unfamiliar skill or task. At the start of and end of your day leave some time for interaction with staff members for socializing and getting to know the culture and the people you will be working with. Starting out with good relationships during the "honeymoon" period will pay off greatly later. While you are still new, use the people who you work with as a valuable information resource. There are all kinds of little things that your employer will not tell you up front but that can be very important. To function optimally a practitioner should know what every co-workers responsibilities are and even better how they do them. Take your time with expressing your viewpoint on controversial issues. Most people need to get to know you before accepting new ideas and opinions.

Be sure to complete all credentialing requirements when starting a new position. Credentialing requirements can include submitting collaborative agreements to your state board of nursing, obtaining Medicare, Medicaid, and third party insurance carrier billing numbers and securing a Drug Enforcement Agency Registration (DEA) number. You must obtain a National Provider Identification (NPI) number as well as a Council for Affordable Quality Healthcare (CAQH) number (AANP, 2013; CAQH, 2016). You cannot bill for services without these documents in place. Practice requirements vary from state to state and it is important to be aware of your state's individual requirements, however billing guidelines are established on a national level. Consider obtaining a copy of your state boards practice guidelines.

References

American Association of Nurse Practitioners (2013). American Association of Nurse

   Practitioners Medicare update. Retrieved from https://www. aanp.

   org/practice/reimbursement/68-articles/326-medicare-update

Center for Medicare & Medicaid Services (2014). Medicare benefit policy manual (CMS

   Publication No. 100-02) Retrieved from http://www. cms. gov/Regulations-and

   Guidance/Guidance/Manuals/ Downloads/bp102c15. pdf

Deering, S. (2016). How to dress for your job interview. *Undercover Recruiter*. Retrieved
from

   http://theundercoverrecruiter. com/how dress your job interview/

Hopf, K. (2014). NP salaries continue to rise. 2014 national salary survey results. *Advance*

   Healthcare Network for NPs & Pas. Retrieved from http://nurse-practitioners-and-
physician-

   assistants. advanceweb. com/Web-Extras/Online-Extras/NP-Salaries-Continue-to-Rise.
aspx

Innes, J. (2012). *The cover letter book: Your definitive guide to writing the perfect cover letter*

(2nd ed.). Great Britain: Pearson Education publishing.

Reeves, E. (2009). *Can I wear my nose ring to the interview? A crash course in finding, landing*

and keeping your first real job. New York: Workman publishing.

Chapter 5

Contract Negotiation and Renegotiation

"Never let your collaborating physician know that you know more than they do about a subject"

The Written Agreements

Business in general and the health care industry in particular functions largely through contractual relationships. A contract is a binding covenant between two or more persons or parties which includes legal terms as is enforceable by law. Fundamentally, a contract is an agreement. This chapter like this whole book is not intended as a substitute for legal or other professional advice but should assist the NP in understanding common contracts and issues in relation to them.

Collaborative Practice Agreement (CPA): Written contract defining the joint practice of a nurse practitioner and physician in a collaborative working relationship within the framework of their scopes of practice. CPAs are required in the majority of states for prescriptive authority.

Elements of a good Collaborative Practice Agreement

    A. The manner in which prescription writing and medication dispensing will be handled

    B. Criteria for procedure performance and specialist referrals

C. Hospital privileges and admission procedures

D. Policies for chart review and co-signing

E. Policies for laboratory, radiology and diagnostic testing

F. Guidelines for patient assignment, triage and on-call

G. Requirements for co-signatures and chart notations

H. Coding and billing procedures

I. Other general medical guidelines and references

Job Description: A job description is a document describing the expectations of any employee for a particular position.

The job description may serve as the basis of performance appraisals by defining the standards of performance related to a particular job. Additionally, the job description can be used to describe a position to a potential job candidate. Duties accounting for more than 5-10% of an employee's time should be included within the job description. The majority of hospitals or large groups who employ nurse practitioners will have a job description in place. In most other cases it will be you researching and providing a job description. Remember the purpose of a job description is to provide written expectations and clarification of duties for a position. Many states require job descriptions for prescriptive authority but beyond this there is no other real legal requirement for a job description. Contact your state board of nursing to determine if a job description is a "must have". Sample job descriptions can be obtained from www.

appexecutives. org.

Employment contract: Business contract setting forth requirements of both the employee

and employer.

An employment contract and a CPA can be one in the same or can be drawn up

separately. The CPA will likely contain more clinical issues while the business contract

contains employment and financial issues. Employee contracts are beneficial to both the

employee and employer. For an employee, the employment contract ensures some

measure of job security. For an employer, the contract may afford protection against

competition in the future. Employment contracts put important issues upfront which

otherwise may not be discussed until particular issues arise later. A written employment

contract is legally binding to both parties.

Most organizations that have already employed nurse practitioners will have an

employment contract to start from. If the employer does not already have an

employment contract then it is suggested that you supply one. The employer will almost

definitely make changes, but by providing your own contract you can make sure all the

issues are addressed that you feel important. Draft the employment contract in a

Microsoft Word format or purchase a software program that will contain all the basics of

a contract to start from. When you are finished with the draft, you may want to seek the assistance of a lawyer to go through it with you. By having a contract in draft form you can save a lot of expensive time spent with the lawyer.

Consider an employment agreement similar to a patient medical record, if it is not documented it has not been done or not agreed upon. Verbal agreements do not hold much weight during legal proceedings.

Elements of a Good Employment Contract

Purpose of the Document

Simply describe who are the employee and the employer in the relationship and the basis of the contract.

Job Description

Describe the services to be performed. In general, this is attached as a separate paper document but referred to as an exhibit.

Hierarchy, Department affiliation

Describe who it is you will be reporting to or who your boss is. At times this may be several individuals such as one person administratively and one person medically.

Duration of employment (Term of the contract)

Describe how long the contract is effective. Some states limit the duration of employment contracts but usually allow at minimum 5 years. There are benefits of having a short-term contract and long-term contract depending on what you feel is most important. A long-term contract may provide you with a feeling of security, but a short-term contract may give you more opportunity for renegotiation in the future.

Alteration and updating the contract

Describe how the contract can be editing or renewed.

Licensure requirements, continuing education allowance.

Describe the necessary certifications or licensure requirements that must be met by the employee and how much money they have to use for continuing education.

Compensation

Describe the amount of money the employee will earn for the position agreed upon.

Employee Benefits

Describe the benefits the employer will provide to the employee during the term of the agreement.

Number of hours per week

The employer and employee may have different ideas of how many hours a full-time position requires if not specifically written. Generally speaking, a full time NP position will require 40-50 hours of work.

Termination Clause

A termination clause specifies circumstances for firing. An agreement to require termination with cause allows the employer to terminate an NP without notice for unprofessional conduct or moral turpitude, felony conviction, drug or alcohol abuse, or loss of licensure. A termination clause including a without-cause action ("at will") allows either party to end the agreement without specific reason. Termination clauses written with a without-cause action can be written with or without a specified notice time (typically 30-90 days) written in the contract.

Practice Dissolution Clause

A practice dissolution clause, often labeled as a "non-compete clause", defines the time period the employee may not work for a competitor of the employer (Brown & Dolan, 2016). Typically a time frame such as 2 years is included along with a geographic radius where the employee may not be employed in a given area of practice. The clause in many cases provides for damages if the covenant is breached (usually $50-100,000) and also provides for financial penalties, typically $1,000 per patient solicited and $5,000 per employee solicited. Non-compete clauses can be complex and are set in place to protect

the employer's legitimate business interests, maintain competitive advantage, and inhibit

confidential information from being exploited (Meseroll, Apatov, & Rutledge, 2015).

Performance Evaluation

Determine how often, by what measurements, and in what manner your job

performance will be evaluated. A performance evaluation is critical to bringing issues to

the forefront. Often people are reluctant to discuss both the good and bad of a person's

performance but without feedback the good may end and the bad will continue because

they go unrecognized.

Contract Negotiation

Negotiation is a problem-solving process in which two or more people discuss their

needs, interests, and differences in an attempt to reach a joint decision often through

bargaining.

Should I hire an attorney?

Nurse practitioners should seek the services of attorneys who are familiar with the laws

and legal issues nurse practitioners face if they are uncomfortable or lack understanding of any topic or issue. Legal fees may be costly but they will likely be worth it in the long term.

Where do I start?

The most important aspect in contract negotiation is preparation. Proper preparation will allow for optimal negotiation, help you decide what is important to you, and will alleviate some of the anxiety of this stressful situation if you have hard facts and figures.

Step 1

The first step in adequate preparation is prioritizing your specific needs. There are four basic aspects to consider: 1) Compensation, 2) Work hours, 3) Benefits, and 4) The amount of autonomy to practice. The greatest error of many employees is to focus on salary and not consider the rest of the contract. Salary is very dependent on work availability and the geographic area but in most circumstances is the major topic of contract negotiation.

Step 2

Consider the other elements of a contract for negotiation rather than focusing only on salary.   Employee benefits may be the best alternative focus of your negotiations.

Benefits are quite costly for employers and may nearly equal compensation in some cases. Key benefits to consider include:

Medical and Dental Insurance. Perhaps the most costly of all benefits, a good medical and dental plan is very important to most individuals and families and will save you a lot of money. The majority of employers will already have a medical and dental plan in place, which may not allow for options. One factor to consider when negotiating is payment of premiums and even deductibles by the employer, which can add up to several hundred dollars every month. Recent surveys show 80-90% of advanced practice providers receive medical and dental benefits.

<u>**Vacation.**</u> Vacation time is another benefit worth negotiating. Establishing a good amount of vacation time early in your career is essential. Employers often don't like extending vacation time later when you become more productive in the practice. Three weeks of vacation has been the average time in salary surveys for the past several years and may be one benefit, which may have slightly decreased, in recent years. Remember time is money and by dividing your salary by 52 will give you a rough idea of what a week of vacation is worth (e. g. $100,000/52wks. = $1,923).

Personal and sick time. These are placed together because they are best placed together in a contract as well. Doing this will allow you to use unused sick time as vacation time. Additionally you can note in the contract that unused sick, personal or vacation time be paid to you in wages at the end of the year or contract period. Do not forget to add in paid holidays.

Malpractice Insurance. We all need this and a good plan may cost up to several thousand dollars. Include this in your contract with premiums paid by the employer.

Continuing Education. As professionals continuing education is important and often essential for certification and licensure. Include not only reimbursement for educational fees but also time off and travel expenses. Over 80% of practitioners receive continuing education benefits in some form or another.

Tuition Reimbursement. If you are considering furthering your education and/or degree and it will benefit the practice then this may be an important factor as well, considering the rising costs of education. Again, the employer may already have a plan in place for tuition reimbursement, however; a contract allows you to further your benefits. Surveys do show a significant degree of increased wages with higher degrees among nurse practitioners.

Professional Dues. Professional dues can add up quickly. These can include licensure fees, prescriptive privilege dues, certification renewals, and membership dues to professional organizations.

Automobile, Subscriptions, Office Supplies, Cell Phones, Computers and Other Practice Supplies. If not in writing it can be an issue. Your idea and the employer's idea of important materials and supplies to practice effectively may differ and become an issue. Putting it in writing gives you and the employer mutually agreed upon guidelines.

Life/Disability Insurance. Approximately half of all practicing NPs have this included in their contract. Yet another key benefit which can be equally important to negotiate in addition to salary.

Retirement. Three-quarters of practicing NPs have retirement benefits. 401k plans and the like are beginning to be strong recruitment tools. Employer's often place restrictions on enrollment such as continued employment for one year. This can be used as a key negotiating tool along with percentage of employer matching into the plan. Employer matching means that the employer will match your contribution into the plan. 401k plans often limit contributions to 10% of your annual salary and employers can match 0-100% of your contribution.

Financial Incentives Financial incentives may include reasonable moving expenses, a sign on bonus, a housing allowance, or payment of educational loans.

Productivity Bonus Some NPs are against the productivity bonus claiming that it may lead to the practitioner seeing patients as numbers and not individuals. This claim has some merit but not enough to change the recommendation for every NP to have a productivity bonus built into their contract. A productivity bonus rewards the practitioner with a percentage of income when set criteria are met. There are multiple ways productivity bonus' can be written. The majority of bonuses are based on revenue generated or number of patients managed or treated. Most employers are not resistant to productivity bonuses since the bonus will only be paid after certain standards are met (usually meaning you are bringing revenue into the organization). Bonuses can also be developed on quality and service metrics.

Step 3

Research. Yes, I know you are tired of research but this will give you the important facts and figures you need for negotiating. Start your research on the web by visiting practice organizations such as those listed in the previous chapters that often contain information on negotiation strategies. Web site such as NP Central (www. nurse. net) and Advance for NPs (www. advanceforNP. com) contain salary and benefit data obtained from surveys of your peers. Local practitioner organizations and practicing NPs may be

willing to give you some idea of salary ranges and benefits among area employers for

comparison. Look beyond the NP role when researching information. Comparing the

costs to employ you versus a new family physician can be very beneficial.

Step 4

Estimate your worth. Estimating your worth includes documenting and discussing your

education and professional experience and perhaps estimating your potential generated

income into the practice or organization. Several simple equations exist which can give

you a good idea of the amount of income you can generate into a practice.

Step 5

Let the negotiating begin. This step will often make you a little diaphoretic. Following

the above steps first will help to strengthen your confidence, alleviate some anxiety, and

allow you to remember what is important to you. Buppert (2013) recommended

following these general guidelines:

- Determine your minimum salary and benefits ahead of time (do not tell them what

  this is).

- Do not be the first to bring up salary. If asked, make statements to put it back on

  their shoulders (e. g. I am much more interested in the position as NP here at

_____ then I am in the initial offer. I will consider any reasonable offer. You are in a better position to know how much I am worth to you than I am.)

- Remember you are on their side, and make certain they know this. An optimal employer/employee relationship will be a win-win situation meaning you will both benefit from the relationship.

- Do not dominate the discussion. Be assertive but not aggressive.

Step 6

Put it in writing. Remember if it is not written it is not legally binding. Do not be the only person to review it. People by nature are more precise when writing than when speaking probably because most of us are better readers than listeners. The act of writing out the agreement also serves to improve communication. Make 3-4 originals of each document so that copies can be provided to the practice, the practitioner, the lawyer, and possibly the board of nursing and/or medicine.

Step 7

Celebrate. Celebrate your new position, new contract, and new partnership. Take your employer and his/her family out to dinner or celebrate on your own.

Salary

Although I believe you should not focus all your efforts on salary during negotiating it still remains likely the most important aspect of employment. Only your salary will pay the mortgage and supermarket bills. Fortunately, the last several years have brought an average increase of 5-10% in salaries. As of June 2015, the median annual NP salary was $104,740 with a range between $70,540 and $135,830. By comparison, the average NP salary in 2011 was $91,310. The hourly pay rate for NPs, regardless of the total number of hours worked per week, was $50. 36. According to the American Academy of Nurse Practitioners (AANP) (2015) and the Bureau of Labor Statistics (2016), NPs in the following states reported the highest average annual salaries:

Hawaii: $115,870

Alaska: $115,670

California: $115,460

Oregon: $111,160

Massachusetts: $107,230

New Jersey: $106,060

New York: $104,510

Multiple factors influence salary, including practice setting, geographic area, degree, and the practitioner's gender. The gender gap is narrowing in our field however and the gap may be partly due to the low representation of men in the profession. Particular practice settings such as emergency care centers and home health agencies are atop the salary list while public health and by no surprise academia round out the bottom. Nurse practitioners with higher degrees will be happy to know that additional education correlates with salary increases. A doctoral-prepared NP can expect to make close to $5,000 more than their Master's prepared counterparts. A few years of experience can also add a few thousand dollars to your salary. As mentioned, the geographic region where you practice may influence your salary as well. The highest paid regions are those that have more difficulty attracting NPs. Areas with an abundance of NPs and NP programs will generally have lower salary ranges. You will also find higher salaries in more urban versus rural settings in most cases. Although salary gain trends have been promising, some experts believe that there will not likely be significant salary gains in the next several years related to extensive focus on cutting costs in healthcare.

NPs are underpaid in comparison to their physician counterparts (see Table 5-1). The cost of providing care to a patient remains the same whether the patient is seen by an NP or a physician. Understand this is a selling point of our services where we can deliver the same quality at a lower cost point and we can join the workforce with less debt in many cases. The average annual salary for a primary care physician is $217,000, which is twice the salary for a NP. This discrepancy equals extra income for the practice. The majority of

NPs are paid guaranteed salaries, which may provide security, but in most circumstances,

results in a lower income. Implementing a productivity-based compensation method can

bring a win-win situation to the NP and their employer.

Table 5-1. NP and Physician Salary Comparison

Nurse Practitioner			Physician Salary*
Clinical Practice Setting	*Base Salary*	*Total Salary*	*Average*
Family Practice	$95,661	$107,917	$217,000
Pediatric	$93,895	$102,493	$209,000
Adult/Internal Medicine	$95,120	$105,922	$262,000
Acute/Emergency Care	**$101,017**	**$111,083**	$322,000

Compensation Programs/ Productivity Formulas

Although salary is a sensitive subject for most NPs it is certainly an important issue

both personally and for the profession. NP compensation methods vary greatly, from

guaranteed salaries, to productivity driven formulas, and even hourly wages. Generally,

while a guaranteed salary may bring you comfort in security, practitioners with productivity-based salaries have higher incomes. Productivity is income based on objective or at times subjective factors such as number of patients seen, hours worked, total charges, net income, other duties such as management activities, or patient satisfaction and/or quality scores (Coombs, 2015). If productivity income is based on collections, which most are, one must consider the net to expense ratio. Most primary care practices have a ratio of 50:50 to 70:30. Expenses which factor into NP compensation include office rent, utilities, salaries and benefits to support staff, medical and office supplies, insurance, and other expenses that come with running a medical practice. Many NPs are unaware of their "Contribution Margin" which is a business term defined as the revenue generated by a provider minus the cost attributed to their efforts (or costs the practice would not have incurred without the provider). Additional factors to consider when determining NP compensation include physician consultation that can be estimated at 5-15% of net income and the risk of doing business involved by the employer also estimated at 5-15%.

Productivity compensation methods encourage higher productivity, than the guaranteed salary but can add to the complexity of determining compensation. Specific circumstances to keep in mind before leaning toward a productivity compensation method include exactly how many patients you would like to see a day, the payer mix you serve, and the collection rate of the practice. Managed care, Medicare, and Medicaid patients tend to be more time consuming and produce less income. If you plan on minimizing the number of patients you see each day (such as <15), you may be better off with a simple guaranteed salary. A good collection rate is at least 90% of billed charges considering your rates are reasonable. Newer NPs should not expect to benefit greatly from a productivity based compensation in their first year of practice but it can still pay off in the long run if you are willing to sacrifice early on.

A good idea may be to attach a productivity bonus to your guaranteed salary contract. This means you can have a set salary and receive additional compensation when certain criteria are met. The bonus can be an increase in base salary when you reach an average number of patients seen daily, a percentage of charges in excess of the income that meets your salary needs, or an overall percentage of net income generated. Don't forget additional sources of income NPs can generate, such as consulting work, research opportunities, and other business ventures.

Keys in Determining Productivity Compensation and Bonuses:

- Use real numbers when determining revenues and put in writing how this information will be gathered.
- Make sure you have access to your productivity numbers or develop a way you can do this yourself. You need to know what you are doing for the practice financially.
- Keep it simple. Sophisticated compensation methods may lead to disagreement. Focus on just one or two incentive methods rather than complicating things with several which take time and money to calculate.
- Become familiar with how you will function in the practice and how this will affect the productivity numbers. Will you be bringing your own patients back, taking their vital signs, and discharging them on your own or will you have assistants to help with the tasks you need not perform.

- Be familiar with the functioning of the "back office". Know who sets up the fee schedules with the practice's major payers, how they respond to denied claims and how they determine the charges.

Renegotiating

Contract renegotiating is not all that different from negotiating your first contract. You still do not want to go into it unprepared. You need to put forth a lot more effort than walking into your physician or practice manager's office and asking for a raise. The steps are similar for renegotiating but at this point you should have a lot more information at your hands.

Step 1

Prioritize your needs. Does your focus remain the same or are you now searching for more time off as opposed to a higher salary.

Step 2

Consider other benefits which interest you rather than focusing on salary. A more flexible schedule, less work hours, extra vacation time, or additional continuing education benefits are all possible requests you can make in lieu of a salary increase. This may be the opportunity to discuss a productivity bonus now that you are likely bringing income into the practice.

Step 3

Research. Do your homework on average salary increases in the area and around the country. Be familiar with your generated income into the practice.

Step 4

Estimate your worth. Reasonably determine what percentage of your generated income the practice should pay you. Your stress level will go down if you have a good set of figures with which to work.

Step 5

Set up an appropriate time with your employer to discuss your contract demands. It is important to have adequate time to focus attention to the topic at hand. Keep a good attitude during your meeting and look toward creating a "win-win" situation.

Step 6

Put it in writing with either an addendum to your old contract or with a whole new contract.

<u>**Successful Negotiation Tips**</u>

- Do your research and always be prepared.

- Have a back-up plan. If the employer does not meet your expectations in one category (salary) then ask for more in another (increased vacation).

- Make sure you talk to the person who is making the decisions.

- Speak with confidence and professionalism.

- Don't blame or accuse anyone for anything.

- Be both objective and reasonable.

References

American Academy of Nurse Practitioners (AANP). (2015). *National nurse practitioner*

compensation survey 2015. Retrieved November 14, 2016 from https://www.

aanp. org/research/reports

Brown, L. A., & Dolan, C. (2016). Employment contracting basics for the Nurse

Practitioner. *The Journal for Nurse Practitioners*, *12*(2), e45-e51. doi: http://dx.

doi. org/10. 1016/j. nurpra. 2015. 11. 026

Buppert, C. (2013). Employment disasters and how to avoid them. *The Journal for Nurse*

Practitioners, *9*(1), 64-65. https://doi.org/10.1016/j.nurpra.2012.11.002

Bureau of Labor Statistics, U. S. Department of Labor. (2016). *Occupational Outlook*

Handbook, 2016-17 Edition, Nurse Anesthetists, Nurse Midwives, and Nurse

Practitioners. Retrieved November 14, 2016 from http://www.

bls.gov/ooh/healthcare/nurse-anesthetists-nurse-midwives-and-nurse-

practitioners. htm

Coombs, L. A. (2015). The growing Nurse Practitioner workforce in specialty care. *The*

Journal for Nurse Practitioners, *11*(9), 907-909.

https://doi.org/10.1016/j.nurpra.2015.06.014

Kane, L., & Peckham, C. (2015). Medscape physician compensation report 2014.

    http://www.medscape.com/features/slideshow/compensation/2014/public/overv

    iew

Meseroll, B. K., Apatov, N. M., & Rutledge, C. M. (2015). The non-compete clause and

    the Nurse Anesthetist: An assessment of knowledge, perception, and

    experience. *AANA Journal*, *83*(5), 329.

    http://www.aana.com/newsandjournal/20102019/noncompete-clause-1015-

    pp329-335.pdf

Chapter 6

Reimbursement of NP's

"Without reimbursement a job becomes volunteer work"

Achieving adequate reimbursement for NP's has been quite costly and difficult. However challenging reimbursement remains one of the key components of justifying Nurse Practitioner existence. As a registered nurse, NP's are well aware how the lack of direct reimbursement negatively influences our value as a profession. Direct reimbursement not only influences professional value yet it allows for the tracking of quality of care measure via payers' databases.

Government Programs

The Health Care Financing Administration (HCFA) has been renamed the Centers for Medicare and Medicaid Services (CMS). The name change according to the DHHS is symbolic of a new focus for the agency, which is directed to being more responsive to the needs of providers and beneficiaries. 1-800-Medicare has also been enhanced to provide 24/7 service and information. CMS has been divided into three separate centers: the Center for Beneficiary Choices, the Center for Medicare Management, and the Center for Medical and State Operations.

Medicare

The Medicare program is in place to provide basic health insurance coverage to the majority of Americans ages 65 years or older as well as individuals who are medically disabled or have end stage renal disease. Medicare is a federally funded program created with the Social Security Act of 1965 and expanded in 1972 and 1973. Medicare is the largest source of health care funding in the United States at this time. In 2011, over 48 million beneficiaries were enrolled in the program, which amounted to over $549 billion in nationwide Medicare benefit payments (Medicare. gov, 2016) . Medicare is divided into two separate programs, Part A and Part B. Part A, is usually provided automatically to people aged 65 and older and to most disabled people. It provides inpatient hospital coverage and includes coverage for skilled nursing services, home health, and hospice care. Part B, which is supplementary, pays particular costs of services provided in an outpatient environment including physicians visits, outpatient hospital services, durable medical equipment (DME) and other services not covered by Part A such mental health services and participation in clinical research studies. However, Part B is subject to monthly premium payments by beneficiaries (Centers for Medicare & Medicaid Services, 2016).

Nurse practitioners were given the right to bill Medicare directly in 1998 with the Public Law 105C33. The law grants payment to NP's regardless of geographic area. Previously, NP's had to bill "incident to" physician's services unless they were distinguished as serving in a rural clinic meeting federal guidelines. Nurse practitioners can bill Medicare directly for services, however they are reimbursed 85% of the physician fee schedule (CMS, 2015).

Obtaining a Medicare number has become easier since the establishment of the Internet, Chain and Ownership System (PECOS) via the CMS website. This option offers an expedited processing timeframe of 45 days versus the 60 day timeframe with the paper application (CMS, 2016).

Medicare used to provide you with both a provider identification number (PIN) and a unique physician identification number (UPIN). The PIN number was used for claims submission and was unique to each site where you practice. The UPIN number is used when ordering durable medical equipment and in some cases when referring to a specialist or other medical service. The Health Insurance Portability and Accountability Act of 1996 (HIPAA as you probably know it) mandated the adoption of a standard unique identifier for health care providers. This is known as a national provider identification (NPI) number and is now often used to track prescriptions as well by provider. On some level it can be thought of somewhat like a social security number as it does not change. At times employers may request this number for you on your behalf but it is recommended that you do it on your own and provide them with the information as you may need easy access your account when adding or changing positions. The idea is that pharmacies and payers will use this number to identify you but this has yet to be truly the case. Groups and employers also have NPI numbers as well for CMS billing.

Nurse practitioners applying to Medicare must hold a national certification and have a Master's degree. Nurse practitioners holding a Medicare number before 2003 are "grand fathered" into the system. Ongoing cuts in provider reimbursement may lead to physicians limiting their acceptance of Medicare patients. Decisions such as this may create a greater need and offer the opportunity for NP's to fill in the gaps and provide care to these clients.

Medicaid (Title XIX of Social Security Act) was initiated by the government to provide health care insurance coverage for individuals in financial need. The federal and state government funds Medicaid. Medicaid is controlled mostly by the state but under federal guidelines. Medicaid was derived to cover very low income. Medicaid is also restricted to families with children, women who are pregnant, or persons who are aged or disabled. The range of services of the Medicaid program includes outpatient and inpatient acute care, diagnostic studies, practitioner services, home health care under certain guidelines, many screening services, and extended nursing care for persons over the age of 21. States often provide Medicaid services within a chosen statewide insurance program. The Medicaid program is overseen by CMS. Certified FNP's and PNP's are covered under Medicaid effective with The Budget Reconciliation Act of 1989 but must apply for a provider number. NP's are reimbursed 100% of physician reimbursement for all services. Applications can be obtained from your state Medicaid program.

Federal reimbursement programs are always secondary to other insurance carriers. This means that Medicare and Medicaid will only be billed charges not covered by the patients other insurance carrier(s), if there is one. Medicaid is always billed secondary to

Medicare. Providers must accept Medicaid payment as payment in full for services rendered. A personal identification number (PIN) is used to bill for services.

DOD Tricare Program / FEHBP

Department of Defense (DOD) TRICARE program, previously referred to as CHAMPUS or The Civilian Health and Medical Program of the U. S, is an insurance program that primarily covers military and their family members. Similarly, the Federal Employees Health Benefit Program (FEHBP) provides health benefits to federal employees and their dependants (U. S. Office of Personnel Management, 2016). NP's are covered under the DOD Tricare program as well as FEHBP (U. S. Department of Veterans Affairs, 2016).

"Incident to" billing

"Incident to" is a billing term utilized by CMS term to describe the billing of NP services incident to or under the direction of a physician. Certain requirements must be met to bill "incident to" a physician including but not limited to (CMS, 2016):

- The NP must be employed or leased by the physician they are billing "incident to". The NP must be rendering follow up care.

- The physician does not need to be physically present in the examination room, however must be present in the "office suite" to assist the NP as necessary.

- If you are addressing a new diagnosis, you cannot use "incident to" billing.

- If you are making a medication adjustment, you cannot use "incident to" billing.

- If the physician has never seen the patient you cannot bill "incident to".

- Services may not be provided in a hospital setting.

"Incident to" billing limits the autonomy of the NP therefore it may not make sense to submit a claim under "incident to". Nonetheless, "Incident to" billing allows for 100% reimbursement of the physician rate while billing directly under the NP provides only 85% of the reimbursement by Medicare and a few third party payers (CMS, 2016). Billing "incident to" when the service provided does not meet the guidelines is considered Medicare fraud. It is important to remember that there is no such thing as billing "incident to" in a hospital setting.

Shared Services

Billing shared services relates to two providers (such as an NP and an MD) sharing in the provision of a professional service on the same day when they are in the same group practice. Likely adopted to compensate for the inability to bill "incident to" in the hospital setting and to take into consideration the occasion when patients are seen as a team. Only one of the providers submits a claim and is remunerated (CMS, 2016). CMS does not provide much clarity on shared services thus the interpretation of what they do provide is frequently interpreted in a variety of ways.

The Nurse Practitioner and practice manager have three options when billing Medicare: 1) Bill all services by the NP under his/ her own Medicare provider number. This decreases the likelihood of fraud but automatically accepts 85% reimbursement of the physician rate on all Medicare cases. 2) Billing services "incident to" in cases where services meet the "incident to" criteria. 3) Billing as a shared service whereas only one provider (NP or more frequently the physician) bills for the services provided by both the providers. The latter methods increase the risk for fraud to occur but allow some of the visits to be reimbursed at 100% the physician rate. The decision is up to the providers and practice managers to make. Certainly, billing "incident to" can increase reimbursement rates but if there is not a good system in place to make sure that "incident to" really is "incident to", then the practice may be better off billing under the NP number. Private insurance may not provide guidelines for the "incident to" billing method, therefore it is important to review their organization's contract.

Private Health Insurance

Despite many recent changes, private insurance organizations continue to provide the major source of health care funding in America. The 2015 National Health Interview Survey demonstrated that 65. 6% of individuals under the age of 65 were covered by private health insurance (Centers for Disease Control and Prevention, 2016). The majority of large employers offer health insurance as a benefit to their employees through private insurance companies. There are well over 1000 private insurance companies in the United States. Most provide fee-for-service reimbursement which increases the financial risk of health care providers.

Indemnity Insurance

The more traditional form of private health insurance companies, indemnity plans pay providers on "fee for service" basis. Health care services are generally paid on a "usual and customary" basis where certain procedures or visits are paid a set fee that is often based on an average charge in the area for the same service. The charge submitted by the provider really does not matter because they will pay the same standard fee no matter what price you are detailing on your claim. If you are in-network then the patient cannot be charged the remainder of the cost as the practice must accept what the indemnity plan pays. Copayments are still collected from the patient. Indemnity plans are not involved in the delivery of care.

Managed Care Organizations (MCO's)

Managed care consists of the integration of delivery and financing of health care. Health plans such as HMO's and PPO's provide members prepaid access to health care at a lower cost. In theory, managed care is designed to foster the effective and appropriate monitoring of a populations health.

PPO's

Preferred provider organizations (PPO's) attempt to provide health care at a lower cost to beneficiaries (those paying for the plan) by offering lower insurance premiums. A PPO plan is a form of MCO plan that uses a provider network to render care. Providers who choose participate with and are accepted into the plan are reimbursed at discounted rates. Providers may choose to join such a plan in order to increase their volume of patients, offsetting the discounted rates. The higher degree of flexibility of PPO plans has put them into the majority of MCO's.

HMO's. A health maintenance organization (HMO) is a form of MCO that offers health care to participating members for a fixed and prepaid amount or premium with the contract that members must see networked providers. Providers who choose to be a networked or participating provider receive prepaid payments to care for a group of enrolled patients for a specific range of comprehensive services. The provider thus shares some of the risk of the HMO hoping their group of patients remain healthy or utilize less health care services. Enrollees are usually assigned to receive health care services from a designated primary care provider.

EPO's . Exclusive provider organizations (EPO's) limit their members to receive health care from its network of providers. Care received outside of the network is not covered except in some emergent situations.

MSO . A managed services organization (MSO) is an organization that performs the enrollment, claims processing and management services for enrolled health plans. MCO premiums have been escalating rapidly in the last few years as the public is expressing desire for less restrictive MCO plans such as PPO's. Because the insured person has only a small amount of financial burden associated with their health care, they have not felt the need to pressure insurance companies further to keep rates low.

Managed Care Terms

Capitation: The prepayment for health care services to providers on a per member basis occurring most often on a monthly basis. Reimbursement remains the same regardless of the costs incurred when caring for the members.

Copayment: The out of pocket medical expense paid by the insured at the time of the visit.

Coinsurance: The amount paid by the insurer when a plan limits its coverage by a percentage. 80 percent is often the limited amount leaving 20 percent to be paid by the insured.

Deductible: A deductible is the amount the insured must pay "out of pocket" before any insurance coverage begins to apply. Deductibles may range from $100 to $3000.

Contracting with MCO's

Managed care has penetrated the majority of the United States overseeing the health care services for a large number of Americans. Contracting with MCO's has become more of a necessity than a choice for health care providers. The historical goal of MCO's to provide access to high quality care has been clouded by its goal of providing cost effective care. Before joining MCO's, the NP or provider group must determine whether the negotiated rates are worth the financial risks associated with capitation.

Essential steps to take before signing on as an MCO provider include:

- Obtain specific cost data and statistical information in order to make an informed decision. Negotiate rates fairly. [SEP]

- Clarify ambiguous data and contract details. Seek a "Win-Win" situation.

- Read the contract in its entirety. Be sure your name will be on the directory and not listed under your collaborating physician's name.

Although a minority, some MCO's choose not to credential NP's. However, this is more likely attributed to a low number of actual applicants. A few health insurers argue that they can't impanel NP's since they are not allowed to practice independently. They do not understand the differences between independent practice versus collaboration mandates. MCO reimbursement to NP's is often done through a supervising or collaborating physician making NP's invisible in the system. If you are providing services under your collaborating physician's identification, then seek to add to the MCO contract language that states services may be provided by the physicians or NP.

References

Centers for Disease Control and Prevention (2016). Health insurance coverage.

  Retrieved from http://www. cdc. gov/nchs/fastats/health-insurance. htm

Centers for Medicare & Medicaid Services (2015). *Medicare information for advanced*

practice

  registered nurses, anesthesiologist assistants, and physician assistants. Retrieved from

  https://www.cms.gov/Outreach-and-Education/Medicare-Learning-Network-

  MLN/MLNProducts/Downloads/Medicare-Information-for-APRNs-AAs-PAs-Booklet-

ICN-

  901623.pdf

Centers for Medicare and Medicaid Services. (2016). "Incident to" services. *MLN*

Matters.

  Retrieved from https://www.cms.gov/Outreach-and-Education/Medicare-Learning-

Network-

  MLN/MLNMattersArticles/downloads/se0441.pdf

Centers for Medicare & Medicaid Services (2016). *Internet based PECOS.* Retrieved from

  https://www.cms.gov/Medicare/Provider-Enrollment-and-

Certification/MedicareProviderSupEnroll/InternetbasedPECOS.html

Medicare. gov (2016). How is Medicare funded? Retrieved from https://www. medicare.

gov/about-us/how-medicare-is-funded/medicare-funding. html

U. S. Department of Veterans Affairs (2016). Veterans choice program: Access health
care

closer to home. Retrieved from http://www. va. gov/opa/choiceact/for_providers. asp

U. S. Department of Veterans Affairs (2016). VHA office of community care. Retrieved

from http://www. va. gov/purchasedcare/programs/dependents/champva/index. asp

U. S. Office of Personnel Management (2016). Special initiatives: Self plus one. Retrieved

from https://www. opm. gov/healthcare-insurance/special-initiatives/self-plus-one/

Chapter 7

Marketing You and the Practice

"Businesses that are thriving and growing have a steady flow of repeat and referred customers. And they get those customers by attracting them rather than pursuing them. Learn their secret for attracting clients here" Michael Beck.

Many practitioners falsely assume that once they open their doors or start their new position the patients will start lining up at the door; after all everyone will become ill at some point in time or need preventive care. Many do not consider marketing to be an important aspect in a medical practice. Others feel as though they are unable to market their practice to achieve the volume of patients they desire. Marketing becomes even more important for the NP provider when the public is less familiar with them than a physician.

The 4 P's of Marketing

Product, price, place, and promotion, otherwise known as the 4 P's, have long been the standard elements in any marketing course, lecture series, or marketing analysis. The first step in any marketing plan should be to establish the 4 P's of your practice. It is often best to establish your 4 P's through the eyes of your patients or guests to your practice.

The first P stands for *product*. The NP's product is the clinical service he or she provides to the patient. Right? Well yes, but try to think of your product as "health and wellness" with a healthy dose of customer service. In order to compete in health care,

NPs must differentiate their product by communicating the benefits of NP care from that of other providers. A well-known benefit of NP care is the focus on the promotion of health and wellness as opposed to physicians who often focus on the treatment of disease and illness. Highlighting shared decision making in collaboration with the patient is beneficial for your product. Additionally, by developing a niche, you can further differentiate your services (such as combining both traditional and non-traditional medicine) (Beck, 2016).

Price, the second P, not only refers to the cost of services but also the proper utilization of healthcare services and total cost effectiveness in providing the services. Compare your price structure for services to your competitors and if your price is lower than this should be communicated to your potential consumer base (Beck, 2016).

The third P is *place* or the geographic location and physical structure of where you practice. The right location of a practice can have a huge impact in your popularity and referral base among potential clients. Before opening a new office or moving to a new location the site should be investigated thoroughly; including a full marketing analysis outlining internal and external threats. Key factors in choosing a site include the location of competitors, the location of the population you are hoping to serve, office availability, accessibility, available financing or resources, and the "not to forget" aesthetics of the place (Beck, 2016).

Promotion, the fourth P is the ability to communicate your message to potential clients. Through the use of promotional modes such as advertisements, a website, a social media page, word of mouth testimonials and referrals, and community presentations. The ultimate goal is to increase the community's awareness of your practice. One of the biggest mistake NPs make in marketing is not placing enough effort and money into their promotional efforts; however, never forgetting that a large percentage of new patients come from established patient referrals and word of mouth (Beck, 2016).

Tracking Return on Investment

To accurately determine positive and negative marketing efforts, it is essential to utilize a tracking program or system. It does not have to be a complex tracking program; a simple program will do. The key ingredient in a marketing tracking program is to document how new patients become familiar with you and your practice. The perfect time for this to occur is when the patient is scheduling their first visit or during their first visit. Do not let a new patient leave your office after the first visit without having asked how they came to you. After developing an adequate tracking plan you can use the results to track return on investment (ROI). Return on investment simply stated is the amount of money returned to you in comparison to the amount of money you put forth in the endeavor. For, example if you paid $200 for an advertisement that resulted in 10 new patients the ROI would be very good. Considering that each new patient to a primary care setting will generate at least $60-$100 at the initial visit and perhaps several thousand dollars over time, this would translate into a positive marketing effort. Tracking ROI will allow you to accurately identify good and poor marketing strategies. This information will tell you where to put your marketing money and effort (Meeks-Sjostrom, 2012).

Seven Simple and Economical Marketing Efforts to Bring in New Patients and Keep Existing Patients

1. Ask your patients for referrals

At first this may be uncomfortable to do. However, don't give up. Once you start and stay with it the more comfortable it will be for you to have this conversation. Start with your patients who come in overjoyed with what you have done for them. If they come in not satisfied or with unresolved symptoms, don't ask them. When you find that delighted patient say something such as, "Well I am glad we have things well controlled now, you know, if you know of anyone else with similar problems send them in; I'd love to help them as well". This is only a few seconds of conversation but can do a great deal with the amount of ease they feel with sending you someone. This small step will undoubtedly increase your number of word-of-mouth referrals by over 15 percent (Meeks-Sjostrom, 2012).

2. Recognize every patient referral

Thank your patients, colleagues, and friends for every referral they give you. Recognizing each referral they give will actually motivate them to send you more. Not recognizing them will make them stop referring to you because they will feel as though you don't need their help or are not thankful of the business. You can thank them in several ways but you should always thank them in person either at their next visit or with a phone call. The phone call should ideally occur soon after the referral comes in. Follow up your personal thank you with a quick handwritten card or small gift. You may want to save the gift giving for the point where they have sent you 2 or more referrals. You should develop a list of those who have referred to you and how many referrals they have sent you. Gradually increase the value of the gifts you give to them with each referral they send you. For example after receiving 3 referrals from the same person send them a small useful gift such as a nice letter opener with your name on it. Stay away from flowers and candy that have no lasting value. When they send you the 4th or 5th referral then send something with value such as a gift certificate to a fine restaurant. If someone goes beyond this then don't be afraid to spend $50-$ 100 on concert tickets or perhaps a large plant for their home or office. All of this may sound expensive but one new patient who stays with your practice can generate thousands of dollars while with your practice (Meeks-Sjostrom, 2012).

3. Develop new patient orientation communication

Send your scheduled new patients a kit containing information about your practice reinforcing the need to keep their appointment with you and making them aware of the services you offer. The kit should contain at a minimum a welcome letter but can also include a brochure, business card, map to the office, marketing resume, and journal or newspaper articles about your practice. Have the front office staff put these together and email or mail one out every time a new patient is scheduled. This simple step will decrease your new patient no-shows and will make them more familiar and comfortable with you at their first visit. You can also have this information available on your practice website (Stacey, 2016).

4. Utilize a marketing resume

A marketing resume is quite different from a traditional resume or curriculum vitae. A marketing resume is intended to promote you to customers that are unfamiliar with you. A marketing resume should include some things traditional resumes do not, such as your picture and perhaps a discussion about your hobbies and family if you are comfortable with this. This information automatically makes you more personable to your patients. A marketing resume also includes the traditional information such as your training, certifications, published literature, research interests, awards, community projects etc. Remember when writing a marketing resume that you are not speaking to an employer but instead a future customer. The marketing resume can be utilized in the following ways: a) included in your new patient orientation communication, b) handed to the new patient by the front office staff before the patient is brought back to see you, c) handed out during lectures or at symposiums, d) available on your practice website, and/or e) left out in your waiting room lobby. The simple steps in developing and using a marketing resume will increase your credibility and likeability with your patients (Stacey, 2016).

5. Develop a recall system

A recall system is set up to remind your patients to return for their follow-up visits. An adequate recall system actually needs to involve 5 key steps.

1. The first step will be the discussion you have with the patient during the visit. This involves explaining to the patient the importance of the next follow up visit ("It is important for you to be seen in 6 months so that we can assure you are on the correct dose of the medication") (Westgate, 2012).

2. The second step is having the front office staff assist the patient set up their next appointment while they are paying their co-pay or going through the discharge process in your office. Setting up an appointment before they leave the office will improve the likelihood of a timely follow-up (NOTE: SETTING AN APPOINTMENT TOO FAR IN ADVANCE MAY INCREASE YOUR "NO-SHOW" RATE) (Westgate, 2012).

3. Step three involves a reminder postcard mailed or emailed, at least two weeks in advance of the appointment. This step can be done by hand or via a software system (Westgate, 2012).

4. The fourth step consists of a telephone call just one to two days in advance of the appointment by your office staff or by an electronic system or a text reminder via the patient's cell phone. Not everyone is good at keeping an appointment book and this step can cut your no shows in half. Most patients at this point are assured to show up at their visit or at least will reschedule their appointment if something unexpected arises (Westgate, 2012).

5. The fifth and last step involves reaching out to those clients who have missed their follow-up visit or have canceled and not rescheduled. Many of these patients may feel the appointment is not necessary or feel they don't have time for the visit. The art of bringing this patient back in to see you lies in stressing the importance of the visit. For example, a patient with hyperlipidemia fails to follow—up at their requested 6-month visit. A personally signed letter by the healthcare practitioner is sent to the patient stressing the importance of the visit ("It is important for us to measure liver function tests to assess for potential side effects from your medication") a week or two after their appointment was due. This letter can be mailed and/or emailed in an attempt to reach the patient. This step can be repeated in another 1-2 months if the patient continues to not make it in. You may also decide to hold refills on their medications until they make their return visit and a note in the letter explaining the risks of side effects without proper monitoring (Westgate, 2012).

6. Develop professional stationary

Whatever the size of your practice a professional stationary presentation can make your practice seem larger. Your stationary should communicate your services and/ or benefits of your practice to both your patient and referrers. Components of a stationary system minimally should include business cards, envelopes, and letterhead. Add a personal logo to your stationary to establish a brand for your practice. A brand gives your practice a trademark or a key identifier. Utilize your stationary with all correspondence including recall letters, referral letters, and letters to friends or colleagues. The stationary will reinforce the benefits of your practice with each piece of stationary they receive from you. Many marketing and advertising firms can assist with the development of your stationary. Business cards are cheap so use them every chance you get: hand them to all new patients, leave them laying out after a lecture given by you, hand them out to everyone you meet, and put them on bulletin boards at your church and gym (Stacey, 2016).

7. Develop referral relationships with colleagues

Nurse Practitioners do not do this nearly as well as physicians or other professionals. Send referrals to your NP peers who may specialize in another area of practice and in turn they will likely do the same. Relationships such as this are a win-win-win situation. The patient benefits from receiving specialized care and both practitioners benefit from the increase in business. This also works with friends who are not NPs such as a friend who may own a vitamin and herbal shop or an acquaintance who is a chiropractor. An additional strategy may be to advertise each other's products or services in your waiting room, on your web site, or even in a mailing (Meeks-Sjostrom, 2016).

And a few more advanced steps to consider to expand your practice...

Utilize a Practice Web Site

Developing a web site can be simpler than you think with some sites offering to build your site for free in return for using their hosting services. Services are available to complete your website as well. (A great resource for this project is www.rsmultimedia.ca). Hosting is the process of keeping your web site active on the World Wide Web. Keep your site simple with general information about your practice such as location, specialty and philosophy together with links to sites you trust for patients to find accurate information on varying illnesses or prevention. This is another place where you can mention or advertise the business of a colleague in return for their advertising your practice on their site. Put your web site address on your business cards, stationery and all of your advertising material. A web site can be easier to remember than a phone number for a potential client when they are looking to find you at a later date. Remember this when you are choosing your web address so that you keep it simple and easy to remember (Stacey, 2016).

Expand into Social Media

Facebook and other social media options is another option to consider to market your services and connect with your patients. Keep your site professional and consider offering wellness tips and other general information for the public (Stacey, 2016).

Develop a Practice Brochure

Again you can do this yourself or hire an expert (Again, a great resource for this project is www.rsmultimedia.ca). A practice brochure is a somewhat flashy marketing tool that should be designed for the client in mind. Appealing pictures and great testimonial statements should take much of the space rather than general information. The practice brochure should convince the reader you care about their health and they need to come see you. Your practice brochure can be used in direct mailings, or emailing to clients, left out during community presentations, given to key referrers, included on your website, and left in your lobby for current patients to take home (Stacey, 2016).

Have the Biggest Yellow Page Advertisement

This is one case where bigger is definitely better. A good yellow page ad can be the most productive marketing effort you have. Clients will naturally gravitate towards the largest ad assuming the company with the biggest ad is the largest and best in its class. You can take advantage of this even if you aren't the largest in town but it will cost you. Yellow page ads are quite expensive but are reaching a large target audience. Yellow page ads should be constructed to be fairly simple yet get the message across. Remember to track your ROI to determine if the cost is worth the referrals generated (Meeks-Sjostrom, 2012).

Web Ads

As you probably thought as you read the above paragraph, Yellow Page ads are giving way to internet ads. Internet ads such as Google AdWords pop up as certain words are entered into a search engine. They are easily set up and often only charge you when customers click on your ad (pay-per-click) (One great resource for this project is www.rsmultimedia.ca). (Stacey, 2016).

Newspaper Ads

Newspaper ads can also be fairly expensive to run but can have a good return on investment if you are in need of new patients. Remember the audience you will reach with a newsprint ad will generally be over the age of 30, well-educated and middle to upper socioeconomic class. Your ad should be placed in the section more particular to your clientele. For example, if you have an ob-gyn practice then you are better off placing your ad in the leisure and food section rather than in the sports section. A newsprint ad should be similar to a phonebook ad with a simple nature but addressing the benefits of your practice (Meeks-Sjostrom, 2012).

Press Release

A press release is one way to get free coverage in the newspaper. Writing a press release does not guarantee that you will get coverage but it is well worth the effort. Press releases can be written about an aspect of your practice or a new medical treatment or discovery you are interested in. An article in the newspaper mentioning your name or practice can often bring in even more patients than an advertisement. People tend to put more trust into an article than that of an advertisement (Stacey, 2016).

Radio and Television Ads

These are both very expensive and usually will result in poor return on investment. Unless you come across a great deal, it is recommended to stay away from this type of advertising. However, if you are asked to be interviewed on a talk show or by a news crew, jump at the opportunity. This will provide great free coverage for your practice (Meeks-Sjostrom, 2012).

Develop a Practice Newsletter

More time consuming than expensive, a practice newsletter can act as a marketing tool as well as an educational tool for your patients. Write reviews on common illnesses such as those you have just read about in your latest journal. Include in the newsletter any new services or changes within your practice. Sent out quarterly to your patients they are reminded of your services and may pass it on to friends and family. A worker within your practice can be designated for assisting with the development with the newsletter together with your input. The newsletter can be emailed, mailed, put on your website, and left in your office; among other places (Meeks-Sjostrom, 2012).

The "Double Hit" Phenomenon

A potential client is more prone to make a decision to come to your practice if they have seen or heard of your practice in more than one way. Thus, it is important to use more than just one avenue for marketing your practice. For instance, you may meet a person at an event and hand them your business card with your web site listed conveniently on the front. Later, while surfing the web they make a visit to your site where they see you specialize in an area they could use help with (Beck, 2016).

Developing a Marketing Plan

After reading through this chapter and maybe a few other sources on marketing, develop your own marketing plan, specific to your practice and community. There are many software programs to help you do this and make it quite easy (Stacey, 2016).

References

Beck, M. (n.d.). The Secret Formula for Attracting Customers. Retrieved November 10, 2016,

   from http://www.businessknowhow.com/marketing/attract-clients.htm

Meeks-Sjostrom, Diana (2012). *Developing your practice*. PowerPoint Presentation.

Stacey, R. (n.d.). RS Multimedia - Kingston Web Design. Retrieved November 10, 2016, from

   http://www.rsmultimedia.ca/index.php

Westgate, A. (2012, November 10). 7 Ways to Attract New Patients to Your Medical Practice.

   Retrieved November 10, 2016, from http://www.physicianspractice.com/marketing/7-ways-

   attract-new-patients-your-medical-practice

Chapter 8

The Basics of Coding and Billing

"When the administrators talk about improving productivity, they are never talking about themselves."

It is recommended that you have both a CPT® and ICDC10 coding book available to reference while reading this chapter.

Coding is the term used to describe the process of assigning identifying codes to the services and procedures we perform and the diagnosis we use to describe symptoms or illness. The American Medical Association (AMA) developed the CPT® (Current Procedural Terminology) codes, which provide a recognized language describing the medical, surgical, and diagnostic services physicians and nurse practitioners provide. The Medicare Catastrophic Coverage Act of 1988 mandated the use of ICD-10 (International Classification of Diseases, 10th revision, Clinical Modification) codes to describe diagnosed illness, symptoms, or health screening (Schuman, 2015). Coding is now the universal language in billing for medical services for the physician and nurse practitioner as well. Many nurse practitioners would like to see our own set of codes based more on the preventative services nurse practitioners provide. In reality, however, for now we will have to stick to the universal codes that lead to reimbursement.

ICD-10 Coding (Diagnosis Codes)

The ICD codes (now on its 10th edition) were first written by the World Health Organization to classify morbidity and mortality information. The codes were expanded for use in the hospital setting and now the U.S. Department of Health and Human Services and the Centers for Medicare and Medicaid Services (CMS) provides a version ICD-10-CM that is more precise. The ICD-10-CM classification system was developed by the National Center for Health Statistics (NCHS) as a clinical modification to the ICD-10 system developed by the World Health Organization (WHO), primarily as a unique system for use in the United States for morbidity and mortality reporting (Schuman, 2015). Although ICD-10 recently replaced ICD-9 for use in coding in October 2015, ICD-10-CM implementation was postponed many years until legislation to replace ICD-9-CM, volumes 1 and 2 with ICD-10-CM was approved. The ICD-10-CM version is used in most clinical settings and is updated every October by the CMS. The revisions to ICD-10-CM included:

- Information relevant to ambulatory and managed care encounters

- Expanded injury codes

- Creation of combinations diagnosis/symptom codes to reduce the number of codes needed to fully describe a condition

- The addition of 6th and 7th character classifications

- Incorporation of common 4th and 5th character classifications

- Classifications specific to laterality

- Classification refinement for increased data granularity

- Addition of placeholder "X"

The ICD-10 codes are well recognized by third party payers including Medicaid and Medicare. In fact, the codes must be used in most situations for claims to be accepted. Several publishers put out a listing of the updated codes annually and a variety of online resources exist and it is essential for every office to have access to these. You should have a copy for yourself and be well familiar with how to look up codes. Many payers are now requiring certain ICD-10 codes be listed for the ordering (or at least payment) of diagnostic testing (*CD-10-CM*, 2016).

The process of coding has become more and more difficult and confusing since there are more and more diseases and illnesses that we are discovering or naming. Medical coding and billing has become a specialty of its own and a specialty certification is even offered. The difficulty in staying abreast of coding and billing issues is that they are ever changing and soon there will be ICD-11 codes to relearn. You can hire the best of coders but the truth is that the provider is always responsible for the coding in legal matters. All providers should have a good working knowledge of the coding system and if you have someone else doing your coding you should be familiar with what they are doing.

Understanding the ICD-10 Code Structure

The ICD-10 codes classify and arrange diseases and injuries into grouped categories. The ICD-10 code set can have three, four, five, six, or seven characters. The first three characters of the ICD-10 code designate the category of the diagnosis. The next three characters (characters three through six) correspond to the related etiology. The seventh character represents one of the most significant differences between ICD-9 and ICD-10. The seventh character provides information about the episode (initial, subsequent and sequela encounters) of care for obstetrics, musculoskeletal, injuries, poisonings, and other external causes of injuries (*CD-10-CM*, 2016; Schuman, 2015).

All ICD-10 codes will begin with a letter of the alphabet (except the letter U). It is important to note that the alpha characters are not case sensitive. The most commonly reported diagnoses begin with the following three characters:

A00 - B99: Infectious and Parasitic Diseases
C00 – D49: Neoplasms
D50 – D89: Neoplasms, Blood, Blood-forming Organs
F00 – F89: Endocrine, Nutritional, Metabolic
F01 – F99: Mental and Behavioral Disorders
G00 – G99: Nervous System
H00 – H59: Eye and Adnexa
H60 – H95: Ear and Mastoid Process
I00 – I99: Circulatory System
J00 – J99: Respiratory System
K00 – K95: Digestive System
L00 – L99: Skin and Subcutaneous Tissue
M00 – M99: Musculoskeletal and Connective Tissue
N00 – N99: Genitourinary System
O00 – O9A: Pregnancy, Childbirth and Puerperium
P00 – P96: Certain Conditions Originating in the Perinatal Period
Q00 – Q99: Congenital Malformations, Deformations, and Chromosomal

Abnormalities

R00 – R99: Symptoms, Signs and Abnormal Clinical and Lab Findings

S00 – T88: Injury, Poisoning, Certain/Other Consequences of External Causes

V00 – Y99: External Causes of Morbidity

Z00 – Z99: Factors Influencing Health Status and Contact with Health Services

Codes longer than 3 characters always have a decimal point after the first three characters. The first character is alpha. Characters 2-7 can be alpha or numeric (*CD-10-CM*, 2016).

The ICD-10-CM is divided into two main parts: the index -an alphabetical list of the terms and their corresponding code, and the tabular list-a sequential alphanumeric list of codes divided into chapters based on body system or condition. The tabular list contains categories, subcategories and valid codes (*CD-10-CM*, 2016; Schuman, 2015). The codes may also contain some use of abbreviations you may need to become familiar with (e.g. *NOS* stands for Not Otherwise Specified or *NEC* stands for Not Elsewhere Classifiable).

The ICD-10 code for the primary reason for a visit should be listed first. Subsequent codes can then follow this code for other conditions or problems that were addressed during the visit.

For example: A patient comes to see you for ear pain and during your examination you discover an acute serous otitis media. During the visit, you also discuss the patient's benign essential hypertension and recommend lifestyle modifications.

The visit may be coded using the following ICD-10 codes:

H65.2 Acute serous otitis media

I10 Essential hypertension benign

If you are uncertain of a diagnosis or need further investigation, then you should not use a

diagnosis code but a code that describes the presentation.

For example: A 12-year-old boy and his mother came to visit you for a chronic cough and

periodic wheezing. You are suspicious for asthma but do not have enough information to

make the diagnosis yet. You order pulmonary function testing and a chest x-ray to rule-

out asthma or other conditions and have the child return the next day.

The visit may be coded using the following codes. The code for asthma should not be

used since you are just ruling out (or in] this condition.

R05 Cough

R06.2 Wheezing

Completing the CMS-1500 Form

The Centers for Medicare and Medicaid Services (CMS) -1500 form, formerly known as

Health Care Financing Administration (HCFA) -1500 is the form used to bill Medicare,

Medicaid, and third party insurers although nowadays this is mostly done electronically.

The CMS-1500 form has space for up to twelve different diagnosis codes per claim.

However, only four diagnosis codes are allowed per charge. For example, if your claim

has one charge, then only four diagnoses codes may be reported. If your claim contains

more than one charge, then more than four diagnoses codes may be reported.

Each procedure or service that you perform should be represented by an ICD-10 code that substantiates that procedure.

CPT® Coding (Services and Procedures)

The American Medical Association (AMA) has developed the uniform coding system known as CPT coding. All reimbursable provider services have a CPT code and all insurance carriers recognize the CPT codes. The purpose of the CPT code is to provide a recognized language in describing medical, surgical, and diagnostic services that allows for easy communication between providers, patients, and third parties such as the insurance industry. In other words, CPT codes describe what was done during the visit. The CPT codes with multiple editions since their inception in 1966 and are revised to some degree annually (AMA, 2015).

The use of CPT codes allows for an adequate and simplified reporting of services or procedures to Medicare, Medicaid and third parties for reimbursement. The CPT code is a numerical five-digit code. The CPT codes are separated into groups as follows:

- Evaluation and Management: 99201 - 99499
- Anesthesia: 00100 – 01999; 99100 - 99140
- Surgery: 10021 – 69990
- Radiology: 70010 – 79999
- Pathology and Laboratory: 80047 – 89398
- Medicine: 90281 – 99199; 99500 - 99607

E&M (Evaluation & Management) Codes

The E&M codes are the "bread and butter" codes for nurse practitioners because they are the codes used most often. The E&M codes describe the professional services of evaluating and managing symptoms or disease (Goldsmith, 2013). In other words, this is the service in which you examine the patient, take a history, and formulate a diagnosis and treatment plan. Although the E&M codes are the most frequently used CPT codes they can be the most difficult to learn. Become familiar with both the 1995 and 1997 versions of the CMS documentation guidelines easily obtained at www.cms.gov.

Breaking Down the E&M Codes

The E&M codes are separated into several categories such as office visits, hospital visits, consultations, and others.

- Office or Other Outpatient Services: 99201 - 99215
- Hospital Observation Services: 99217 - 99220
- Hospital Inpatient Services: 99221—99239
- Consultations: 99421 – 99255
- Emergency Department Services: 99281 – 99288

The categories are then divided into subcategories.

e.g. Outpatient Services

- Established Patient: 99211 - 99215

The subcategories are then further classified into levels.

e.g. Outpatient Services

- Detailed Established Patient Office or Other: 99214

Selecting the correct E&M code

The process of selecting the correct E&.M code increases in difficulty as you further define the code.

Step One. Start first with selecting the location of service. In most cases this will be in the office or an outpatient setting (99201 - 99215).

Step Two. Next determine whether the visit is with a new patient (not seen by anyone in your group in the past 3 years) or established patient. Most nurse practitioners' patients will fall under the established patient category 99211—99215 in the office setting. (No distinction is made between new or established patient in the emergency department setting.)

Step Three. The last step is the most complicated. This involves selecting the level of service that is appropriate for the visit. There are five different levels of services that are defined by the degree of complexity of the visit in an outpatient office setting and can simply be defined as limited, basic, expanded, detailed, and comprehensive. The degree of complexity is based on several factors including history, examination, medical decision making, counseling, coordination of care, nature of presenting problem, and time. The history, examination, and medical decision making are the key features used in selecting a code while the other factors can be considered contributory (the exception to this are visits which consist predominately of counseling).

History

The extent of the history obtained is determined by the provider in relation to the presenting problem for that visit. For example, a less extensive history is needed on someone presenting with a finger laceration as opposed to someone presenting with chest pressure. The extent of the history obtained can be defined by four categories:

Problem focused: Consisting of a chief complaint and brief history of present illness.

Expanded problem focused: Consisting of a chief complaint, brief history of present illness, and a problem specific review of systems.

Detailed: Consisting of a chief complaint, an extended history of present illness, a problem specific review of systems with review of a few other systems, pertinent past, social, and/ or family history which relate to the problem being addressed.

Comprehensive: Consisting of a chief complaint, extended history of present illness, comprehensive review of systems pertinent to the problem addressed with the addition of the review of all other systems, and a complete past medical, family and social history.

Examination

The extent of the examination is also determined by the provider, based on the presenting problem. The examination can be classified into the same 4 categories:

Problem focused: Consisting of a limited examination of the injured or affected area.

Expanded problem focused: Consisting of a limited examination of the affected area and other related systems or areas.

Detailed: Consisting of an examination of the affected area and extended to other affected areas or related areas or systems.

Comprehensive: Consisting of a general multi-system examination or complete examination of the affected organ system.

The CPT coding guidelines recognize the following as systems or areas to be examined: Head-Neck-Chest-Abdomen-Genitalia-Back-Extremities-Eyes-Ears, Nose, Throat, Mouth-Cardlovascular-Respiratory-0Gastrointestinal-Genitourinary-Musculoskeletal-Skin-Neurologic-Psychiatric-Hematologic, Lymphatic, Immunologic (Goldsmith, 2013). It is important to keep this in mind during your documentation process.

Time

Time can also be used as a factor in determining the level of E&M code that you use. This can be difficult. The documented time must be the time spent face to face with the provider and should be described in nature (such as coordinating home health care or counseling regarding diet and lifestyle change in relation to hypertension).

Limited >15 minutes, Basic >30 minutes, Expanded >40 minutes, Detailed >60 minutes, Comprehensive >80 minutes

Medical Decision Making

The degree of medical complexity is also divided into four categories: straightforward, low complexity, moderate complexity, and high complexity. Selecting the medical decision making complexity level is based on three factors: the number of diagnoses or management options, the amount or complexity of data to be reviewed by the provider (medical records, diagnostic tests, etc.), and the risk of significant complications or morbidity/mortality. To qualify for a given level of decision—making, two of the three elements must be met at the same level or exceeded (Goldsmith, 2013). For example, to meet the criteria for moderate complexity decision making, then at least 2 of the following 3 elements must be met or exceeded: a moderate level of risk, a moderate amount or complexity of data to be reviewed, and multiple diagnosis or management options.

Selecting the appropriate level of E&M code is also based on the categories and subcategories already defined.

For example, in relation to office visits: A new patient office visit will require that all the key components including history, examination, and medical decision making meet or exceed the requirements to qualify for a level of E&M service. Thus, for a detailed E&M

level (99204) to be met there must be a comprehensive history, a comprehensive examination, and medical decision making of moderate complexity. However, if the patient was an established patient then only 2 of 3 of the key components must be met. Thus, for a detailed E&M level (99214) two of the three following must be met; a detailed history, a detailed examination, and moderate complexity decision-making.

Realize that this is the most difficult area of coding to grasp and there is not always agreement on the level of E&M codes. The complexity of decision-making can be somewhat of a subjective measurement since there are not specific measurable criteria for level of risk or complexity of data to be reviewed. A pocket-sized worksheet may be helpful or if you are more techno savvy handheld software applications are available as well. You should be familiar with your use of the different E & M levels. Most primary care providers will have a bell curve look to their E&M patterns with mostly level 3's, a lot of level 2's and 4's and a few level 1's and 5's. It can be helpful to compare yourself to other providers in the same clinic or specialty especially if you tend to see similar patient types.

Use of Procedure Codes

Use of the other CPT codes are easier to select and simply consist of finding the right CPT code to identify the procedure, which was performed. For example, if during a well-child exam, you gave an IPV immunization you would include the CPT code 90713 (Poliovirus vaccine, inactivated, for subcutaneous use). Once you become familiar with codes you commonly use you can make yourself a pocket card or place them on your "Superbill". A superbill serves as a receipt for your patient and sort of a charge slip for your office. Most offices will have these if they are not yet computerized.

Modifiers Mayhem

While there are thousands of CPT codes to use for the reimbursement of services, it's the modifiers that can add the extra detail and reimbursement for a visit. A modifier serves as an addendum to CPT codes and indicates that the service or procedure has been altered in some way. In other words, it further defines a service. The CPT code must still accurately define the procedure or service performed, the modifier just says something is different than usual. For example, the C25 modifier applies when a significant separately identifiable service is performed by the same provider on the same day of another procedure or service. For instance, a patient is in your office for an annual exam and you noticed an unusually shaped lesion, which you remove during the visit. You can bill for the appropriate E&M service and for the lesion removal procedure by attaching the C25 modifier. Without adding the modifier most payers will bundle the two separate services assuming the procedure was part of the exam and thus resulting in a lower reimbursement. Other examples include when a service or procedure is performed more than once during the visit (modifier C59) or when two different surgeons are performing two distinct parts of the same surgery on a patient the same day (modifier C62).

Unlisted Procedures or Services

When a procedure or service is performed that does not have a CPT listing then there are a few code numbers that can be used to bill for the procedure/service. The code should then be followed by an explanation of what was done. The majority and maybe all the services or procedures you provide will have their own number. If there is no code, then look for an unlisted code located in the section where you would find the procedure or service if there was a code. One example is code 90799 described as *Unlisted therapeutic, prophylactic or diagnostic injection.*

Completing the CMS-1500 Form

CPT codes are listed in section 24 of the CMS-1500 form. The diagnosis (ICD-10) code, which relates to the procedure (CPT) code should be linked by placing the ranked number of the ICD-10 (1, 2, 3, 4) in the box entitled "diagnosis code" located next to the CPT code box. Section 24 contains room for 6 separate CPT codes (CMS, 2015).

CMS Common Procedure Coding System

The Common Procedure Coding System was added in 1983 by Health Care Financing Administration, which we now call Centers for Medicare and Medicaid Services (CMS). The purpose of CMS was to standardize codes for Medicare processing that are not located in the CPT manual. Technically the CPT codes fall under the heading of the CMS coding system labeled Level 1 but it is simpler to think of them separately. The CMS coding system is divided into three levels including the CPT codes as level 1, the level II codes pertaining mostly to supplies, materials, and injections, and the level III codes which allow the local Medicare carriers to identify services that are to a certain area. Note that not all of CMS codes are covered by Medicare. The CMS level II codes are organized in a similar fashion as the CPT codes and consist of a 5-digit alphanumeric code including a letter followed by 4 numbers (CMS, 2015). The following is a listing of the various sections in the CMS level II coding publications.

Transportation services: A0000 – A0999

Medical & Surgical Services: A4000 – A8999

Miscellaneous and Experimental: A9000-A9999

Enteral and Parenteral Therapy: B34000-B9999

Temporary Hospital Outpatient: C0000-C9999

Dental Procedures: D0000-D9999

Durable Medical Equipment: E0000-E9999

Procedure/ Services Temporary: G0000-G9999

Rehabilitative Services: H5000-H5999

Drugs Administered other than Oral Route: J0000-J8999

Chemotherapy Drugs: J9000-J9999

Temporary Codes for Durable Medical Equipment Regional Carriers: K0000-K9999

Orthotic: L0000-L4999

Prosthetic Procedures: L5000-L9999

Medical Services: M0000-M9999

Pathology and Laboratory: P0000-P9999

Temporary Codes: Q0000-Q0099

Diagnostic Radiology Services: R0000-R5999

Private Payer Codes: S0000-S9999

Vision Services: V0000-V2999

Hearing Services: V5000-V5999

The Most Important Lessons in Coding Documentation

The single most important lesson about billing and coding is to adequately document what it is you do. Nurses are trained from the start about the importance of accurate medical documentation and it can help us both financially and legally now in the nurse practitioner profession. Documentation is the only evidence that payers must show what was done and whether what was done is supported by medical necessity. Correct billing documentation is just as important as traditional medical documentation when it comes to medico legal issues.

Do Not Up-Code

J. R. Ewing from the well-acclaimed show "Dallas" once stated that "Once you lose your integrity the rest comes easy". So, maintain your integrity.

Up-coding is the term used for billing at a higher level of service than that performed or billing for services never done. Not only is this plain un-ethical it is illegal. Nurse practitioner providers will likely receive even more scrutiny than their physician counterparts during an audit. Never, ever, ever up-code. The most frequent area where up-coding is found to occur is with the E&M codes. Always make sure your documentation and the care you provide supports the level of E&M code selected.

Do Not Down Code

Down Coding is the term used for billing for a lower level of service than that provided. Most nurse practitioners are more apt to down-code for the fear that they may accidentally up-code. Billing for a lower level of service can be as drastic as the above by decreasing practice income and thus not justifying your role. If the visit meets the guidelines of a certain level and this is well documented, then the visit should be billed at that level. Many practices have resorted to just billing all their visits at a certain level thus minimizing insurance carrier scrutiny, but this is not good practice. First, billing all visits at the same level often triggers an audit. Second, billing at one level will not guarantee insurance carrier automatic payment.

Do Not Ignore the Subject of Coding

You may feel confident that you have qualified coders who work for you but don't use this as an excuse not to learn the coding process. The provider (that's you) is the responsible party for assuring the coding is done correctly. Ignorance is not an appropriate excuse when fraud occurs. Your knowledge of coding and billing issues will increase your worth to the practice. Very few physicians enjoy this aspect of practicing medicine as well.

Always Be as Specific as Possible

Code to the highest level of specificity possible with ICD-10 codes and CPT codes.

Link Your Codes

Be sure to link tests/procedures ordered or performed to an appropriate ICD-10 code. This will help justify the reason for the test/procedure (CPT code).

Use All the Resources Available

Computerized coding and documentation systems will pay for themselves and allow you to be more productive and spend more time with your patients. Don't be afraid to consult your coding manuals especially with diagnoses and codes less familiar to you.

Perform Ongoing Internal Audits as these audits can catch potential problems. If performed prior to billing, audits may save you from generating false claims and may increase your revenue by catching under-coding.

References

American Medical Association. (2015). *CPT 2016 Professional Edition*. Chicago, Ill

CD-10-CM expert for physicians 2017: The complete official code set. (2016). Eden Prairie,

MN:

   Optum360°

Centers for Medicare & Medicaid Services (2015). Medicare Claims Processing Manual

   Chapter 12 - Physicians/Nonphysician Practitioners Retrieved from https://www.

   cms. gov/Regulations-and-Guidance/Guidance/Manuals/Downloads/clm104c12.

   pdf

Goldsmith, H. (2013). E/M Coding: Medical decision-making in the making:

   evaluation/management. *Podiatry Management*, *32*(5), 46.

   http://www.podiatrym.com/

Schuman, A. J. (2015). ICD-10: What you need to know. *Contemporary Pediatrics*, *32*(3),

   40-42. http://contemporarypediatrics.modernmedicine.com/

Chapter 9

Building a Solo Practice

"Not only believe in miracles but rely on them."

The African Impala

   The African Impala is a wonderful deer like animal residing in Southern Africa. Although the Impala does not look that much different from a deer, other than its peculiar antlers, it has tremendous capabilities. In a single leap the Impala can jump over 8 feet high and 30 feet long. Despite this great leaping ability, the Impala can be easily contained in a zoo environment.   The Impala is often contained with nothing more than a three-foot high fence. The zookeepers know the Impala can easily jump over this fencing but the Impala chooses not to. Why is it that the Impala chooses not to leap over the fencing? Because the Impala must be able to see where it will land before it leaps. The Impala lacks faith and is unwilling to take the risk of leaping where it is not sure where it will end up landing. The Impala would never choose to be in a solo practice because it lacks the entrepreneurial quality of risk taking. Webster's Dictionary defines an entrepreneur as "one who organizes, manages, and assumes risk of a business or enterprise".

   Building a solo practice is not an easy task for the physician let alone the NP. Multiple barriers exist for the clinician initiating such an endeavor. Receiving lower wages and reimbursements have made it harder for nurse practitioners than physicians to sustain a primary care practice (Chapman, Wides, & Spetz, 2010). Foremost, nurse practitioners have yet to gain the respect they deserve as independent providers, which often results in inadequate reimbursement by insurance providers and public ignorance of what nurse practitioners do. Making this process even more difficult some states where nurse practitioners have full practice authority they still face barriers getting paid for their services. Insurance companies are refusing to reimburse nurse practitioners directly without a physician or do so at a much lower rate than physicians receive for the same services (Yee et al. , 2013). Additionally, over half of all new businesses in the United States fail in the first year and a half and of those who do survive the first year % fail within the next five years.

This chapter is not only written for the nurse practitioner considering starting an independent practice but for those who work as employees as well. Having a knowledge of the process of initiating and maintaining a business will give you respect for all that is involved. There are currently well under 2% of NP's who actually own their own practice.

Are You Ready to Start Your Own Practice?

Even though Nurse practitioners have been practicing successfully over the last 30 years in primary care and rural settings physicians are opposed to giving nurse practitioners full practice authority. Physicians argue that nurse practitioners lack education and this causes nurse practitioners to be unqualified and unsafe to practice solely unsupervised which is a major barrier (Clarin, 2007). Research has shown that Nurse Practitioners are safe competent health care providers and are sometimes preferred over their physician counterparts. \As hundreds of thousands of people gain access to health care through the Affordable Care Act many states are allowing nurse practitioners to practice independently without the oversight of physicians. As of today 21 states including the District of Columbia have full practice authority. Full practice authority allows nurse practitioners to practice to the fullness of their degree and scope of practice in their state. Full practice means the nurse practitioner can assess, diagnose, and prescribe medications independently. Here is a list of those states where nurse practitioners have full practice authority: Alaska, Arizona, Colorado, Connecticut, District of Columbia, Hawaii, Idaho, Iowa, Maine, Maryland, Maine, Minnesota, Montana, Nebraska, Nevada, New Hampshire, New Mexico, North Dakota, South Dakota, Oregon, Rhode Island, Vermont, Washington and Wyoming (AANP, 2020)

Whether you are prepared to start your own business will likely rely on several key issues including your financial situation, personal life situation and the degree of determination and motivation you have. Starting an independent practice is certainly not for everyone and you must really be willing to take a significant degree of risk. Weighing the pros and cons of working independently versus working as an employee is a process we all go through at least in our heads. Some may come to a conclusion with minimal thought when faced with the uncertainty of how well a private practice may do. Others

may want to take more time to think and even write down the strengths and weakness of

independent practice to determine if they are ready to take the plunge. Consider the

sacrifices you may have to make as a small business owner, the risks involved with starting

a new business venture, the support system you have in place, and the special skills you

have that may set you apart from the other providers in your area. A helpful task during

your decision process may be to write down the pros and cons of independent practice as

you see them against each other.

PROS	Independent Practice	CONS
-Independence		-Security
-Flexibility Demands		-Administrative
-Chance for Higher Income		- Benefits

Business Formations

Choosing a business form

Care should be taken when deciding which corporate form to utilize while operating

your business venture. Many experts recommend consultation with a lawyer or certified

public accountant to assist with this decision. Business forms are usually categorized as either informal or formal with the differentiation often being that formal associations require the filing of organizational documents with the Secretary of State. Most successful practices end up as a corporation but this does not mean you have to start as one. Your first decision on a business formation does not have to be your last one. Many small businesses start as sole proprietors then change to a formal business entity once the business has been established. There are some states that require a certain type of entity be set up and this typically can be found on the state secretary of state website. A brief review of the various formats follows.

Informal Associations

Sole Proprietorship: One person who conducts business for profit. The sole owner assumes complete responsibility for all liabilities and debts of the business. The income of the business is reported as part of the owner's personal income.

General Partnership: Two or more individuals as co-owners of a for-profit business. Partnerships should operate under a written partnership agreement to avoid future problems. All partners are responsible for the liabilities and debts of the partnership. Partnerships enjoy single taxation like sole proprietorship. Income is reported as part of each partner's personal income.

Formal Associations

Limited Liability Partnership (LLP): A general partnership, which elects to operate as an LLP. To operate as an LLP, a registration must be filed with the Secretary of State. Unlike a general partnership described above, the partners in an LLP enjoy protection from many of the partnership's debts and liabilities. The income of an LLP is taxed in the same manner as a general partnership.

Limited Partnership: A partnership with at least one general partner and one limited partner. A limited partner's liability is limited to the amount invested, while the general partner(s) assumes all the liabilities and debts of the partnership. The income is taxed in the same manner as a general partnership.

Corporation: A legal entity, which is created by filing articles of incorporation. The Corporation itself, assumes all liabilities and debts of the Corporation. A Corporation is owned by shareholders. A shareholder enjoys protection from the corporation's debts and liabilities. There is an option of having just one shareholder. Income is taxed twice, first at the corporate level and then the employee level when a wage is paid or at the shareholder level when distributed as a dividend.

S-Corporation: After filing articles of incorporation, a Corporation may seek to obtain S Corporation status, for federal income tax purposes. The income of an S Corporation is taxed only once: at the employee or shareholder level. To qualify, the corporation may not have more than 75 shareholders and must meet other certain Internal Revenue

Service criteria. The Corporation must submit IRS form #2553 to the IRS. An S Corporation is considered a corporation in all other aspects and is subject to no additional or special filing requirements with the Secretary of State.

Nonprofit Corporation: A corporation whose purpose is to engage in activities, which do not provide financial profit to the benefit of its members. Such corporations must obtain nonprofit or tax exempt status from the IRS and State Department of Revenue, to be free from certain tax burdens.

Limited Liability Company (LLC): An LLC is a formal association, which combines the advantage of a corporation's limited liability and the flexibility and single taxation of a general partnership. An LLC has members, rather than shareholders. A member enjoys protections from the liabilities and debts of the LLC. Although not required by law, an LLC should operate under an Operating Agreement much like a Partnership Agreement. If the LLC qualifies under IRS guidelines, it may be taxed only once, like a partnership, at the employee or member level while not having the same restrictions as an S- Corporation.

Surveying the Market

The demand for your services must be present if your business is going to succeed. Determining whether there is a demand for your services should be done before your decision to go into independent practice. Before beginning an analysis of your target market you should have already developed an idea for your intended services. That is, what is it that you intend to provide or sell. You may decide to open a practice focused on your training such as family practice, women's health, pediatrics, or geriatrics. You may also decide to specialize in the care of certain disease entities such as diabetes, obesity, or fibromyalgia. The basis for your decision should not only reflect your interests but also the market where you intend to practice.

In order for your business to survive in the market area you wish to establish your practice the area must be able to support another practice or be inadequately supported by the existing practices. A survey of your potential market can be done in several different fashions and should not rely on only one.

Window Survey

A window survey is just as it sounds, surveying a particular area through the window of your car. Grab your local phone book (or do a quick online search) and a map of the area you wish to serve. Next drive around your potential market area surveying the established practices and marking them on your map. When you are finished visiting all the existing practices then visit the areas that are absent of an existing practice and evaluate whether there is a need for the practice you wish to establish.

Census data reviews

Your local librarian can assist you with reviewing the census of zip codes in your area. This information can be very helpful together with your window survey in determining heavily populated areas where no current practices are located.

Develop a Strategic Plan

Establish in your mind where you want your business to be. Once you have determined that an independent practice has potential and are committed to realizing your dream then your first step should be to start planning.

Find a mentor

Finding someone who is already running their own practice who can give you the much needed advice that you will need to start and run your practice is key. Having a mentor will not only help you to avoid pitfalls, it will help you decide if this is the route that you really want to take. Start with making calls to your local clinics, find someone that is doing something very similar to what you want to do in your own practice.

Writing a "Business Plan"

Successful businesses begin with the development of a comprehensive business plan. A business plan serves multiple purposes and is a must for every business. Foremost, the business plan serves to establish the direction you take during start up and will make you address several key areas of business development you may otherwise avoid addressing.

A good business plan is also essential in acquiring loans and relaying your goals to the accountants, lawyers, and anyone else you will work with.

The process of writing your business plan may involve the assistance of an accountant or lawyer but the first draft should be done by yourself. Only you know how you want your business to look and function. The actual writing of the plan can be directed by reading one of several books on the subject or with the use of business plan writing software. .

Business Basics

Selecting a Name for Your Business

Law requires that the name of a Corporation, L. P. , L. L. C. and an L. L. P. must be distinguishable from the names of other businesses of the same type. Search the web site or call your state's Secretary of State office for information on name checks or applications to reserve names. You may also want to seek consultation with an attorney who specializing in copyright law. The name of your practice should distinguish you in some way from other practices and at the same time tell the potential customer what it is you do. Common errors in developing a name include making the name lengthy or complicated. Keep your name short and easy for the consumer to understand. Run your name by several lay people as well as medical professionals before you make your decision. Your name will be hard to change once you have begun to practice and establish your business.

Continuing Responsibilities

After its initial organization, formal businesses must continue to meet certain statutory requirements. Requirements will vary by state and you should seek direction from a good CPA (certified public accountant) who you will likely need at some point in the process of starting a new business. You might as well start at the beginning stages.

Marketing

Marketing in today's business world is not an option even among professional corporations. Many business plans include a section for marketing but this is one area, which deserves a separate plan and focused attention. An important aspect for the independent nurse practitioner is establishing a niche or unique focus that will grab the attention of your potential clients. Use this unique aspect of your practice in developing a sales pitch. A sales pitch says "why you" in one brief statement. An example of a sales pitch for the business described in the sample business plan is "Caring for You with the Balance of Alternative and Traditional Medicine".

Accounting

A good accountant is a must but the majority of the checks and balances will likely be performed by you or your business manager (if you have one). Again you can and should make use of available computer programs. A good accounting program is well worth the small investment and makes the process of "keeping the books" simple (appexecutives. org). All good accountants are familiar with these programs and it will make their job easier as well when it comes to tax time.

(Collaborative Agreements) Hiring Professional Services of a Physician

It is imperative that nurse practitioners establish a collaborative relationship with a physician and all members of the healthcare team to address the need of a growing population (IOM, 2011). Most states require nurse practitioners collaborate with a physician to practice. Independent nurse practitioners will then have to establish a relationship with a physician and likely pay them for their services. For instance, it may be required that a physician review at least 5% of your records where treatment was prescribed. You can set up a contract where you pay the physician for each chart reviewed or pay them a monthly fee for reviewing your charts.

Research the current laws and practice acts in your state and seek legal counsel. It is important to find a lawyer who is knowledgeable with nurse practitioner practice.

Licenses

Your business will likely need to apply for an Employer Identification Number (EIN), which serves to identify you as an employer. Many banks require this number to open a business account and often times businesses you work with will use this number to establish accounts with your business. The EIN is used for tax purposes most importantly and can be obtained online or by phone quite easily. Additional licenses you may need to set up include:

Clinical Laboratory Improvement Amendment (CLIA) Certificate of Registration. If you will be performing any sort of laboratory work within your office setting (including CLIA waved testing) you will need to register with CLIA. There are different levels of registration dependent upon the complexity of testing you plan to do within your practice. Information can be obtained off of CLIA's web site (www. fda. gov/cdrh/clia).

Biohazard Waste Generator Permit. You will need to check with your state office as to whether this is required. You will most definitely need to establish a relationship with a hazardous waste company to pick up and dispose of the hazardous waste that is generated (unless the medical office you lease already has this in place for you).

Federal, State, and local licenses

Check with your local Chamber of Commerce with regard to which licenses may be required for you to be open for business in your practice location.

Essential Forms

HCFA 1500, Patient intake, Initial HIP, Prescription pads, Telephone call forms, Consent forms, Visit forms, Superbills, Patient instruction handouts. Of course some of those forms can be eliminated with an electronic medical record some of which are free.

Essential Reference Books

Physicians' Desk Reference, CPT, ICD-10, Diagnostic Reference, Primary Care Reference, Emergency Care Reference. Again all of which you can get electronically in this day and age.

Billing for Services

There are several ways to set up billing for your services. You will have to make the decision of whether to set up relationships with third party payers in order to receive payment from I-IM0's, PPO's, Medicare, Medicaid and other health insurance organizations. It is always a good idea to accept private pay patients, which gives you payment at the time of services (that is unless you want to set up payment plans with patients).

Accepting Private Pay

Credit Card Acceptance

Credit cards increase sales and increase the size of the sale while it cuts down on collection problems. People have become accustomed to using credit cards for payment, which makes it essential for you to accept them. In order to accept payment via credit cards you will have to set up a Merchant Account with a bank. Preferably you can do this at your own bank but you may need to research a few others to compare costs. The majority of banks charge a set-up fee and then a monthly fee that may correlate with the amount of transactions you make. The bank will set you up with a scanner which either works through a phone line or through a personal computer. The Merchant Payment Scanner or Software allows you to run credit cards through to verify validity of the card and then transmission of funds to your account. You will have to decide which credit cards to accept such as VISA®, MasterCard®, American Express®, and Discover®, which are listed in order of most widely used. Agreeing to accept payment from these credit cards means that you agree to accept the discount associated with the particular cards. The discounts range from 3-7% of each transaction dependent upon the amount of the sale, your monthly volume and the particular card. The upside is that your account is credited immediately. Accepting credit cards will increase your cash flow and may decrease your need for expensive short-term loans as you start your practice. You may have heard of some new services that turn your phone or iPad into a scanner. These also charge a fee but often have no monthly fee.

Accepting Personal Checks and Cash

Accepting personal checks also gives you payment quickly but comes with a little risk (the risk of a returned check). Generally speaking, medical offices receive less returned checks than the majority of businesses and it is probably worth the small risk. Accepting

cash is a given in any business but be sure the transaction is recorded accurately. All

patients should be provided with a "superbill" which lists the diagnoses, the procedures

and services rendered, the amount paid, and often times when their next appointment is

due. A "superbill" can be hand generated or computer generated and can serve as a

receipt for the patient. There is a risk to accepting cash as well given the chance of theft

(including employees).

Accepting Third-Party Payment

The decision to accept third-party reimbursement may be determined by the third

party payer. Some NP's in private practice try to just stay away from the "red tape" of

third-party reimbursement and only accept payment at time of service. In order to build a

fair sized practice, however, it may be a good idea to at least investigate third—party

contracts. Medicare and Medicaid very rarely turn down NP providers so start with them.

Establishing Your Rates

An independent nurse practitioner will likely have to be fairly competitive with regard

to their fee schedule. Legally, medical offices should not discuss their fee schedules with

other practices. You will probably have an idea of what the other providers in your area

are charging by the rates you were charged as a patient or by your previous experience.

You can really choose to set your prices how you see fit and you can adjust your fee schedule up and down just so long as you charge everyone the same fees. Medicare lists what they pay for certain CPT codes on their website which can certainly be a starting point. Many practices base their rates by multiplying Medicare allowable by a certain percentage such as 125%-200%. Realize what you charge is often not what you get paid by third party payers.

Establishing Your Office Setting

Geographic Location

Geographic considerations are frequently influenced by such factors as family, recreational areas, housing availability, cost of living, and the results of your market survey. Once you have found the general area, which you would like to practice, the search begins to find an office setting.

Office Space

Options on obtaining office space include buying, leasing, or sharing office space. Buying space will not likely be an option for a start-up business unless you have a substantial amount of investment money to start your practice with. Sharing office space can be a good idea so long as the practice you share space with is not a competing business. Sharing a space may allow you to begin part-time until you establish patients and are able to afford leasing a full-time office. The advantages of leasing include having an identified office of your own and the ability to construct or renovate it the way that works best for your practice. The most important aspects of choosing an office will be the location, costs, and the functionality and current condition of the facility. Consider having a lawyer review any lease or agreement you are considering.

Office Supplies

There are multiple equipment and supply needs for a medical practice. The majority of these materials will be needed before you open your practice doors. Many of your equipment and supply needs can be purchased as used or donated by yourself or others. Essentials will include at least one personal computer, several phones and phone lines, a fax machine, furnishings and medical supplies. Group purchasing associations exist to get better rates and require yearly or monthly membership fees.

Financing

Determining Start-Up Costs

Starting a new practice involves a substantial amount of start-up money. You may or may not have enough money of your own to get your practice started. Generally speaking, the costs associated with starting an independent practice will be more than you expect. Before seeking funding for your new business you should have some idea of the initial start-up costs and average monthly expenses. It Is very difficult to estimate or know how much will be needed to fund your new business but an effort should be made to look at all the expenses that you are aware of.

Obtaining Start-Up Funding

Many new businesses begin with funds from their own bank account but this is not always possible unless you have been planning and saving for some time. Small loans can be obtained from local or international banks as well as through the Small Business Administration (www. sba. gov). Research your funding options before you sign the papers on a large loan with a large annual percentage rate and seek the consultation of your accountant.

Keys Step toward Success

Provide quality care

To become a successful solo practitioner, the most important practice is to provide high-quality patient care. Keep up to date in your field by attending conferences and reviewing appropriate journals on an ongoing basis.

Be a patient advocate

The deliverance of superior care that is proven through outcomes requires being an outspoken patient advocate. Your ongoing journal reading will lead to treatment modalities that you would not have thought of before which will end up benefiting many of your patients.

Be available and accessible

Availability and accessibility are reliable practice builders that will also improve the care you provide. Be available to see new patients within 24 hours. Patients should know they can reach you in 20-30 minutes at all times so make that easy to do or provide for alternatives. You can always send emergency situations to the emergency room but patients like talking to their own provider (first if that) option is available to them.

Provide personalized care

Personalized care is always a top priority. Patients appreciate that you know them personally. On the same hand they usually connect with you better if they know you personally. A good start is by including a picture of yourself on a marketing resume and including your hobbies or interests allowing them to connect with you on a more personal level. Conversing with them about events in your own life reminds patients that you are human. Discuss something personal during every visit showing your interest in him or her as a whole person. Don't forget to truly listen to your patients. Two minutes of active listening will create a better relationship with your patients than ½ an hour spent of you talking.

Provide cost-effective care

As a sole practitioner you can provide better continuity of care with increased cost effectiveness.

Provide "outrageously great service"

Truly great service is from the heart. Be aware of and ask about service breakdowns in your office. When you discover a problem then fix it by looking at the patient's perspective first and foremost.

Have a sense of humor

A good sense of humor and a positive attitude will go a long way. Don't forget to allow your staff to have an appropriate amount of freedom to have fun at work as well.

Create a Unique "Niche"

If you are the only person in the city specializing in fibromyalgia, then make it well known. Creating a Niche market is a great strategy that will not only bring in more clients into your practice, it will help to decrease barriers for nurse practitioners, reduce healthcare cost and improve healthcare outcomes for patients overall (Naylor & Kurtzman 2010).

Management Mastery

Learning effective management skills is not an easy process and one that may not be possible to learn without experience. Including significant management techniques in this book would add another 100 pages but here are a few key important ingredients.   Hire the right people and treat them well. Your employees will become your business' greatest asset if you train them and treat them right.

Pay attention to the numbers and details. Do not rely on others to make sure all the checks and balances are correct and in order. As a business owner this is your responsibility.

The more attention you pay to a behavior the more it will be repeated. Accentuate the positive.

Make informed decisions based on both quality and cost. "Market to grow". You must market intensely as you start your business and never stop marketing as it grows. Marketing works, that's why we do not have to pay for local television and radio.

Dress in business attire. Dress like a professional to be respected as a professional.

Ask your happy patients for their referrals. Never underestimate the power of a patient referral. People usually trust their friends over an article, ad, or even a respected journal article.

Catch employees doing things right instead of naturally catching them doing wrong.

Health plan enrollment. To gain access to patients, many practitioners choose to enroll in all available plans. On the same note make sure you read and understand every detail of a contract.

References

American Association of Nurse Practitioners. (AANP) (2013) Nurse Practitioner State

Practice Environment, retrieved from https://www.aanp.org/legislation-

regulation/state-

legislation/state-practice-environment

Chapman, S. A. , Wides, C. D. , & Spetz, J. (2010). Payment regulations for

advanced practice nurses: Implications for primary care. *Policy, Politics, & Nursing*

Practice, *11*(2), 89-98. https://doi.org/10.1177/1527154410382458

Clarin, O. A. (2007). Strategies to overcome barriers to effective nurse practitioner

and physician collaboration. *The Journal for Nurse Practitioners*, *3*(8), 538-548.

https://doi.org/10.1016/j.nurpra.2007.05.019

Institute of Medicine (IOM). (2011). *The future of nursing: Leading the change,*

advancing health. Washington, D. C. : The National Academies Press

Naylor, M. D. & Kurtzman, E. T. (2010). The role of nurse practitioners in

reinventing primary care. *Health Affairs,* 29(5), 893-899.

https://doi.org/10.1377/hlthaff.2010.0440

Yee, T., Boukus, E., Cross, D., & Samuel, D. (2013). Primary care workforce

shortages: nurse practitioner scope-of-practice laws and payment policies. *National*

Institute

for Health Care Reform. Research Brief, (13) Retrieved from

http://nihcr.org/analysis/improving-care-delivery/prevention-improving-health/pcp-

workforce-nps/ .

Chapter 10

Corporate Compliance / Malpractice

There is never a situation where you should say "I'm new at this".

Corporate Compliance

The federal crackdown on Medicare fraud and abuse has invoked fear of an audit for many practitioners and physicians. The sample compliance program for small practices released by the Officer of Inspector General (OIG) lists seven key components of a compliance program. The OIG recognizes that the scope and size of an organization may limit its resources for establishing and maintaining a compliance program. The OIG still expects smaller practices to make some effort to establish a compliance plan. You should not assume that the size of your practice will protect you from an investigation. The following seven key components are meant to be recommendations and practices are not required to take the advice. The components include:

• Conducting internal monitoring and auditing.

• Implementing compliance and practice standards.

• Designating a compliance officer or contact.

• Conducting appropriate training and education.

• Responding appropriately to detected offenses and developing corrective action.

• Developing open lines of communication.

• Enforcing disciplinary standards through well-publicized guidelines.

(Office of Inspector General, n.d.).

Chart Auditing

Practices that audit frequently may actually realize an economic benefit. Remember that audits catch under-billing just as frequently as over-billing, especially among nurse practitioners. There are other benefits to performing audits such as discovering information you did not see during the visit, catching missed follow up appointments or follow up on lab work and opportunities to make improvements in documentation forms etc. The Office of the Inspector General (OIG) gives no specific recommendation on the frequency or amount of chart auditing that should be performed. However, you need to be aware of your state's guidelines and if applicable your collaborative agreement requirements for the timing and percentage of chart audits that are necessary. The percentage of charts that any given state mandates to be audited can range from zero to 20% annually (NNCC, 2014). The NNCC (2014) has the state by state guidelines available to direct you as an NP to ensue you are in compliance in your specific state. The charts should not be "cherry picked" but chosen in some random fashion. An audit of all charts where a patient had an adverse outcome is also considered good practice. Audits are performed by your collaborating physician per state guidelines and in those states that do not require chart audits the audit can be completed by trained, in-house personnel or by a hired agency.

What is being looked for during an audit?

-Coding and Billing. Services are coded and billed correctly with appropriate modifiers.

-Documentation is completed correctly. Documents are legible and include the reason for visit, relevant history, the exam, testing, diagnosis, plan of care, date, provider identification, rational for testing, etc.

- Basic history information is documented and updated on a regular basis (HPI, ROS, past medical, family and social history)

-The services performed are reasonable, necessary, and documented in the medical record (e. g. there is a proper ICD-10, CPT codes to go along with the procedures performed).

-Improper self-referrals or kickbacks (Meeks, n.d.)

Developing Standards

A practice should initiate a corporate compliance program starting with practice standards and procedures in written form. To start, the standards should determine how records will be selected for audit, how many records will be audited, procedures to take when errors are found, and the performance of staff training. Included in the standards may be auditing tools and procedures for retaining, creating and destruction of records. Additionally, the standards should put in writing the provider's commitment to compliance with all state and federal statutes, rules, and regulations. The standards should be distributed to all employees. A statement certifying the employee has received, read, understood, and has agreed to the standards should be signed by each employee and placed in their employee record.

Designate a Compliance Officer

A compliance officer can consist of one person responsible for the whole program or a committee of people responsible for different aspects of the program. A non-staff member can be designated as the practice's compliance officer however th-s employee must be familiar with clinical activities, billing and coding, and your state's laws and regulations for primary care practice (Shickle, 2015). The duties of the compliance officer include, but are not "limited to":

- Developing the practice's compliance program with policies and procedures that follow the state laws and regulations.

-Overseeing periodic audits.

-Revising the compliance program as needed.

-Developing or organizing staff training in relation to corporate compliance.

-Investigating reports of improper business practices.

-Taking corrective action when errors or improper practices have occurred.

Conducting Appropriate Training and Education

Training and education with regard to corporate compliance should be reoccurring according to the OIG based on your state's guidelines and your collaborative agreement if applicable. Training can be performed in—house by the compliance officer or by outside sources.

Once the audit is completed a post audit meeting should present the following:

-Proper documentation for services rendered.

-Applicable sanctions and regulations.

-The operation and importance of the compliance program along with its benefits.

-Legal sanctions for submitting deliberately false or inaccurate billings.

-Information discovered during the internal audit.

Responding to Detected Violations

The corporate compliance standards should in detail explain the process of responding to discovered violations. The process should include three basic steps: Step one involves the investigation of a potential problem to be sure it truly exists. Step two is correcting the problem identified immediately. The last step is determining whether self-disclosure should occur and whether you contact a lawyer (Shickle, 2015).

In summary, remember that it is the provider who is ultimately responsible and that a good compliance program is a good business decision. A good compliance program will protect you more than hurt you. Encourage employees to notify the compliance officer of potential problems. Be sure employees are aware that their anonymity will be kept as best possible and no retribution will occur for truthful information. Compliance efforts should be coordinated with third party billing services if possible to keep communication open and easy.

Medicare and Insurance Audits

In 1996, a massive government audit of Medicare payments revealed over $24 billion in incorrect payments (Inspector General Audit 1997). As a result of this audit Medicare developed a mechanism, whereby claims are run through a "filtering system" or "audit system" before payment occurs. This filtering system has been successful enough that insurance carriers are beginning to do the same. The internal audit system builds a database or "profile" of each provider which tracks billing code utilization. The program then can identify statistical outliers who are flagged for more stringent audit. Circumstances often raising red flags include the repetitive billing of the same codes, a high percentage of claims for one procedure, an unusual procedure from your norm, and a high number of claims or patients coming from one provider. Other leads that may lead to an audit include problems reported by patients, another provider, employees or even professional whistleblowers.

HIPAA Compliance

The latest regulatory challenge facing providers is the Health Insurance Portability and Accountability Act (HIPAA). HIPAA was enacted by Congress in 1996 when the healthcare industry could not successfully agree to standardization. HIPAA sets forth requirements for the Department of Health and Human Services (DHHS) to coordinate standard transactions and codes for the health care industry. Transactions refer mostly to claims and inquiries while codes refer to the common ICD-10 and CPT billing codes you should now be familiar with.

Realizing that electronic transactions are becoming commonplace, Congress also initiated new privacy provisions as well. The privacy provisions not only cover billing transactions but all healthcare information. The Privacy Rule consists of four major components (U.S. Department, 2003):

1).Consent and authorization

All patients should sign a consent form allowing anyone involved in healthcare operations access to patient information. An additional form must be signed by the patient if medical information is provided for reasons other than the provision of health care services (such as research).

2).Minimum necessary uses and disclosures

This portion of the Privacy Rule states that persons only have access to or access information that is vital to their performance in their health care role. Large organizations should make information inaccessible if possible to those persons who do not need the information. Smaller organizations will likely just be required to initiate policies stating that employees will only access information that is vital to their function instead of initiating costly processes, which actually limit their access.

3).Patient Rights

Patients have the right to access a copy of their record and should not be charged fees except those for copying.   Patients may also request to add an amendment to their record. Providers may refuse this request but will have to follow an extra set of measures. The provider's office must also keep track of all authorized disclosures of the medical record that is available to the patient.

4).Administrative changes

All practices must identify a staff member as a "privacy officer". This could be your "compliance officer" or office manager. All practices must also draft a policy that describes how patient information is handled. Staff must be trained on these issues via policy review or via seminars or training programs. Medical records must be protected in some manner.

Guidelines have been written by the DHHS for providers to follow. The guidelines frequently state that reasonable changes be made giving smaller practices time to comply and realizing limitations of a small practice. The Affordable Care Act of 2010 will further those requirements. Numerous changes are likely to occur as HIPAA evolves and it will be important to stay abreast of the requirements.

Malpractice Issues

The topic of malpractice and professional liability is one that most NP's would rather avoid reading about. Fortunately, however, the number of lawsuits filed against NP's has historically been limited when compared to physicians. In a comprehensive analysis of claims made according to provider-type, Hooker, Nicholson, & Le (2009) found that NP's were roughly 24 times less likely to make malpractice payments than physicians during the same 17 year period. The explanation for this may be related to several conditions including a smaller number of practicing NP's in relation to practicing physicians, the acuity of patients seen by NP's, underreporting of such lawsuits to the National Practitioner Data Bank (NPDB), and the known patient satisfaction with NP care. Also, the majority of claims occur for physicians in "high risk" specialties such as surgery where NP's care is limited. The majority of lawsuits dealing with NP's are due to delay in making a diagnosis, failure to diagnose, failure to treat appropriately, and medication errors (Wojcik, 2014).

For an actual malpractice lawsuit to be valid four particular elements must occur: Duty, Breach of Duty, Damages and Causation

1. The first element is the "duty to provide care" to the person must have been established. In other words, a patient-practitioner relationship must have been established.

2. The second element is the "breach of duty" or failure to provide the standard of care. This can occur either by doing something you should not have or not doing something you should have for the patient.

3. "Damages" or injury to the patient must also occur and this represents the third needed element. The incurred injury usually will have to consist of a physical injury since psychological damages are difficult to prove.

4. Lastly, the injury to the patient must have been directly caused by the breach of duty by the practitioner. (Morales, 2012)

Most medical malpractice cases are settled for a "reasonable" amount out of court. Remember plaintiff attorneys are usually only paid upon winning a case (contingency fee) and therefore are not likely to take a case unless they feel they can win. Defense attorneys are generally paid by the hour. Your best prophylaxis against the filing of a malpractice case against you includes the following important actions:

Communicate, Communicate, And Communicate!! Establish a good rapport with your patients. A patient is less likely to file a suit against you if they trust you and feel as though you care about them. NPs tend to be sued less than their physician counterparts because we spend more time with a patient during each patient encounter.

Remain competent at what you do. Maintain your certification and annual continuing education credits. Be knowledgeable of the standard of care for the conditions you treat (such as by following national guidelines). If something falls out of your realm of knowledge then refer appropriately.

Document accurately and comprehensively. The old nursing phrase of "If it is not documented it was not done" still holds true in the NP profession.

Take a course in risk management. Risk management is a set of techniques or behaviors to reduce your risk of being sued. In essence risk management courses teach you why patients become plaintiffs (Wright, 2012).

.

Court/ Deposition Preparation

Preparing for a court hearing or deposition can be one of the most dreaded tasks for anyone. Adequately preparing for such a daunting event, however, can put you at greater ease. The first step you take should consist of educating yourself on the course of events and standards of care. Review the patients chart first by yourself and then with your lawyer in an attempt to recollect the events that occurred. A precisely documented visit record will certainly make this easier. Review the standard of care for the condition or symptoms you treated at the time of the visit as well. Recommend experts or documents to your lawyer that support your decisions and to improve your credibility. Next, discuss your case honestly and openly with your lawyer so he or she can assist you. It is generally recommended that you refrain from talking to friends, family, co-workers, and the patient or his/her lawyers.

Once the proceedings begin it is important to maintain a calm and professional demeanor at all times. A professional appearance and mannerism is also important and will greatly affect your credibility during the proceedings, so pay attention to detail. Plaintiff attorneys really know how to put on the pressure and will work to use your words against you, so go slow when answering questions. Do not hesitate to ask the lawyers to rephrase a question or even ask for a short break during a deposition.

Professional Liability Insurance

Nurse practitioners malpractice claims are on the rise as more nurses are expanding into the advanced practice role. There are a number of companies that provide malpractice insurance for NP however, in the last few years we have seen a significant rise in premiums for this coverage. While searching for an insurance carrier be familiar with whether the plan is an "occurrence" versus a "claims made" policy (occurrence is usually best), how much coverage you have per claim and aggregate ($1 million/$3 million means a maximum of one million dollars per claim with up to a maximum of 3 million dollars for all claims made against the provider per year), and whether you have a say when it comes to making a settlement (Ullman, 2015). Don't be afraid to ask questions and talk to several companies or representatives.

Types of Liability Policies

All liability policies are not the same. NP's should carefully review their policies annually. There are two main types of policies: occurrence and claims made. An occurrence policy covers NP's for claims arising from medical incidents occurring between the policy inception date and expiration date. So long as the claim pertains to an incident that occurred during the policy period it is covered under the policy. A claims made policy, however, only cover claims that arise from a medical incident during the policy period and also filed during the same period of time. It is thus very important to renew claims made policies with a retroactive date if this is the type of policy you choose. "Tail" insurance may also be purchased to cover retroactive time periods if you choose to cancel a claims made policy (Ullman, 2015).

There is no perfect way to determine how much liability insurance coverage to purchase. Some factors that will need to be considered when purchasing malpractice insurance are

1. Where you work. Consider both your geographic location and your area of specialty

2. What kind of services do you provide? The greater the number of services and procedures the more your chances of being used will increase.

3. What type and how much coverage does your employer provide? Even if you have coverage through your employer you still should have your own separate medical malpractice insurance since you may not be covered if only you are sued.

4. How much with my own coverage cost? Malpractice coverage for an NP to purchase on one's own generally runs around $1,200 a year. This is a wise investment if you want to also guarantee your own separate legal representation (Wojcik, 2014).

Table 10-1: Top Areas of Malpractice Claims Against NPs	
Family Practice	
Adult Gerontology	
Pediatrics and Neonatal	
Obstetrics and Gynecology	
Psychiatric	(Nurse Practitioner 2012 Liability, 2012)

Controlling Liability Premiums

The biggest factor on the medical malpractice insurance industry is obviously the number of lawsuits filed and the amounts actually paid to resolve these claims. The recent wave in large dollar judgments has found many companies with inadequate money reserves leaving them unable to pay off settlements. Several large insurance companies have actually removed themselves from the market. Insurers utilize several assessment tools to determine premium rates in addition to lawsuits filed and amounts paid. One such tool is the review of closed claims where insurers review closed cases to identify allegations per specialty, suits filed with respect to geographic location, amounts paid, and losses related to particular procedures performed. Premium rates thus have little to do with your skills and knowledge as a provider but more to do with the climate of liability within your specialty and geographic location. The current "hardened" insurance market may actually open up discussion with regard to tort reform. Several states have had success in passing tort reform that essentially places caps on damages (Cook, 2013). Without limits, the insurance industry becomes unable to cover its obligations, which then results in unreasonable premium to providers.

References

Cook, A. (2013, January 10).   *Tort reform update: Recently enacted legislative reforms and state court challenges*. [State Courts White Paper].   Retrieved from: http://www. fed-soc. org/publications/detail/tort-reform-update-recently-enacted-legislative-reforms-and-state-court-challenges

Meeks, J. (n.d.). Do I Need to Audit My Charts? Retrieved December 08, 2016, from http://nurse-practitioners-and-physician-assistants.advanceweb.com/Article/Do-I-Need-to-Audit-My-Charts.aspx

Morales, K. (2012). The 4 Elements of Medical Malpractice in Nursing. Retrieved December 08, 2016, from http://www.nursetogether.com/4-elements-medical-malpractice-nursing

NNCC State-by-State Guide to Laws Regarding Nurse Practitioner Prescriptive Authority and Physician Practice. (2014, March). Retrieved December 8, 2016, from http://www.nncc.us/images_specific/pdf/2014StateGuideRegulationsGoverningNursePractitionerPractice.pdf

Nurse Practitioner 2012 Liability Update 20 - HPSO. (2012). Retrieved December 8, 2016, from http://www.bing.com/cr?IG=184759CEF9DA475395A8DA55E5B2F69E&CID=3BD7B7E

C7E65681023BFBE097F5469A1&rd=1&h=Y2HgDYMkGqhRhborWXRUt1XAtD1y8ny2laij

4-

Z0ah4&v=1&r=http://www.hpso.com/Documents/Individuals/Professional%20liability

/NP_Claims_Study_2012.pdf&p=DevEx,5053.1

Office of Inspector General, Department of Health and Human Services. (n.d.). Office of

Inspector General | U.S. Department of Health and Human Services. Retrieved

December 08,

2016, from https://oig.hhs.gov/

Shickle, A. (2015). A To-Do List for Medical Practice Compliance Officers. Retrieved

December 08, 2016, from http://www.physicianspractice.com/blog/do-list-medical-

practice-

compliance-officers

Ullman, A. J. (2015). How Often Are Nurse Practitioners Sued? Retrieved December 08,

2016,

from http://nurse-practitioners-and-physician-

assistants.advanceweb.com/Columns/Legal-

Issues/How-Often-Are-Nurse-Practitioners-Sued.aspx

Ullman, A. J. (2015). Must Haves For Your Malpractice Policy. Retrieved December 08,

2016,

from http://nurse-practitioners-and-physician-

assistants.advanceweb.com/Columns/Legal-

Issues/Must-Haves-for-Your-Malpractice-Policy.aspx

U. S. Department of Health and Human Services, Office of Civil Rights (2003). *OCR Privacy*

Brief: Summary of the HIPPA Privacy Rule. Retrieved from: https://www. hhs.

gov/sites/default/files/privacysummary. pdf

Wojcik, J. (2014). Primary care provider role exposes nurse practitioners to malpractice

risks |

Business Insurance. Retrieved December 08, 2016, from

http://www.businessinsurance.com/article/20140413/NEWS05/304139997/primary-

care-

provider-role-exposes-nurse-practitioners-to-malpractice-risks

Wright, W. L. (2012). Malpractice Prevention. Retrieved December 08, 2016, from

http://nurse-

practitioners-and-physician-assistants.advanceweb.com/Web-Extras/Online-

Extras/Malpractice-Prevention.aspx

Chapter 11

Justifying and Promoting the Nurse Practitioner Profession

"It's the action, not the fruit of the action, that's important. You have to do the right thing. It may not be in your power, may not be in your time, that there'll be any fruit. But that doesn't mean you stop doing the right thing. You may never know what results come from your action. But if you do nothing, there will be no result."
— Mahatma Gandhi

Background: Over 50 years and counting!

Dr. Loretta Ford and pediatrician Dr. Silver began the first official NP educational program began in 1965 at the University of Colorado (Ford, 1997). However, NP's owe the first threads of advance practice nurses of nurses to nurse anesthetists and midwives beginning as early as the 1940's, followed closely by the concept of the clinical nurse specialist (CNS) by Hildegard Peplau (Sheer & Wong, 2008). The U.S. and global role of the advanced practice nurse has continued expanding in duty, scope, and knowledge base. The growth has spurred recognition of international scope and standards of practice and recognition of global barriers to practice (ICN International Nurse Practitioner/Advanced Practice Nursing Network, 2005; Klienpell et al., 2014).

Advanced practice nurses have assisted in expanding healthcare access. However, barriers remain to full practice authority. Many initial barriers to practice arose from within nursing, including difficulty in role identification from acute care and bedside nursing, resistance by physicians, regulating and legislative bodies unaware of the purpose of and how to regulate the role, and confusion by patients (Brown & Draye, 2003).

International barriers mimic these barriers and include complexity and multiple titles for advanced practice nurses, differing educational requirements, differences in education quality per school and country, conflicts in scope of practice by state or country, and unclear role clarification (Klienpell et al., 2014). Although the effectiveness of NP practice and satisfaction by patients is well documented and becoming better known, work remains.

How can the profession be more clearly defined and promoted? Know your own power. You are the profession. Your actions, values, speech, and how you choose to practice convey clear messages to your patients, staff, fellow APRNs, other healthcare providers, legislators, and communities. You are a key solution, both in individual action and involvement in professional organizations.

Nurse practitioners have practiced now for five decades, as we look towards upcoming decades we must ask what we want for our profession, our patients, and ourselves. We will likely face many similar issues and new challenges demanding development of new and different ways to examine and respond to issues. The keys to promoting our profession lie in both our zeal to respond and the flexing of our power in numbers. Promotion efforts by each individual nurse practitioner are vital. Focused attention must be made to legislators, healthcare payers, patients, other healthcare professionals, and most importantly the public. Traditionally, the APRN has been hidden behind hospital or clinic practice walls, hindering public awareness of our existence. We must be proactive in engaging media, who often turn to physicians first for expert information on health topics. Historically, APRN's have done a poor job promoting the profession, busy instead working hard to provide quality care to their patients and having difficulty finding the shift from being a staff employee to taking responsibility as the primary care provider, but you can help turn the tide.

Steps in Nurse Practitioner Promotion and Justification:

Step 1: Know the facts

Nurses are well respected

In Gallup polling of the general public, nurses consistently hold the highest rankings for standards of honesty and ethics than any other profession Over 85% of surveyed Americans report nurses have high ethical standards well ahead of physicians (Gallup, 2016). This survey continues to recognize nurses at the top of the list. The empathetic, knowledgeable, and equitable care nurses provide creates strong respect by the public. Health consumers know they can find a listening ear, sound advice, and a helpful hand from a nurse. The gap between public opinion percentages is something to consider. These same traits are what make APRN practice unique, important, and in demand.

Nurse Practitioners provide quality care

Multiple studies support the quality care nurse practitioners provide. There is a listing of only a few of the prominent research articles outlining effectiveness of NP practice in table 12-1. Strong evidence for the positive impact of NP practice on patient outcomes was recently highlighted in an extensive meta-analysis of existing research (Newhouse et al., 2011). Nurse practitioners met or exceeded physician outcomes in the following areas:

- *Patient satisfaction*: Satisfaction was equivalent to physician comparison groups in all studies analyzed.
- *Ratings of perceived health*: In studies where patients were asked to assess their own health, those cared for by NP's rated their health equivalent to those cared for by physicians.
- *Functional status*: In measures of ability to complete ADLs, patients cared for by NP's rated their functional status equivalent to those cared for by physicians.
- *Blood glucose control:* Blood glucose control in patients cared for by NP's was equivalent or better than those cared for by physicians.
- *Lipid Control*: Control of lipid levels in patients cared for by NP's was better than those cared for by physicians.
  Blood pressure: Blood pressure levels in patients cared for by NP's were equivalent to those cared for by physicians.
- *Emergency and urgent care visits*: Rates of emergency department or urgent care visits were equivalent among patients cared for by NP's and physicians.
- *Hospitalization*: Rates of hospitalizations were equivalent among patients cared for by NP's and physicians.
- *Length of Stay*: Length of hospital stay was equivalent among patients cared for by NP's and physicians.
- *Mortality*: Patient mortality was equivalent among patients cared for by NPs and physicians (Newhouse et al., 2011).

There has yet to be a study showing lower quality of care with NP's in comparison to MD's.

Table 12-1: Studies on NP Practice Outcomes

Article	Findings
Virani, S., Akeroyd, J., Ramsey, D., Chan, W., … Petersen, L. (2016). Comparative effects of outpatient cardiovascular disease and diabetes care delivery between advanced practice providers and physician providers in primary care: Implications for care under the Affordable Care Act. *American Heart Journal, 118,* 74-82.	- Diabetic patients under APRN care more likely to have glycemic and BP control. - Cholesterol control more likely in patients cared for by physicians.
Allen, J., Himmelfarb, C., Szanton, S., & Frick, K., (2014). Cost-effectiveness of nurse practitioner/community health worker care to reduce cardiovascular health disparities. *Journal of Cardiovascular Nursing, 29*(4), 308-314.	- Creation of NP lead Enhanced Usual Care team - At 1 year intervention group had overall improvement in LDL cholesterol, systolic and diastolic BP, and HbA1c - Improvements in the above led to notable decrease in healthcare costs
Collins, N., Miller, R., Kapu, A., Martin, R., Morton, M., Forrester, M., … Wilkinson, L. (2014). Outcomes of adding acute care nurse practitioners to a level I trauma service with the goal of decreased length of stay and improved physician and nursing satisfaction. *Journal of Trauma and Acute Care Surgery, 76*(2).	- Decreased length of stay in patients. - Statistically significant reduction in cost. - Increased satisfaction by both physicians and staff nurses.
Kuethe, M., Vaessen-Verberne, A., Elbers, R., Van Aalderen & W (2013). Nurse versus physican-led care for the management of asthma. *Cochrane Database of Systematic Reviews*, 2.	- Equivalent rates of asthma exacerbations or asthma severity after treatment. - No difference in costs or quality of life for patients.
Gielen, S., Dekker, J., Francke, A., Mistiaen, P., & Kroezen, M. (2013). The effects of nurse prescribing: A systematic review. *International Journal of Nursing Studies, 6.* doi: 10.1016/j.ijnurstu.2013.12.003	- Equivalent or improved clinical parameters. - Equivalent or improved perception of quality of care by patients - Better patient satisfaction
Goldie, C., Prodan-Bhalla, N., & Mackay, M. (2012). Nurse practitioners in postoperative cardiac surgery: Are they effective? *Canadian Journal of Cardiovascular Nursing, 22*(4), 8-15.	- NP patients had higher satisfaction ratings of education and pain management

Peeters, M.J., et al. (2012). Nurse practitioner care improves renal outcome in patients with CKD. *Journal of the American Society of Nephrology, 25*(2), 390-398.	- For the NP intervention group patients had significant differences in blood pressure, proteinuria, LDL cholesterol, use of aspirin, statins, active vit. D, and blood pressure medications.
Morris, D., Reilly, P., Rohrbach, J., Telford, G., Kim, P., & Sims, C. (2011). The influence of unit-based nurse practitioners on hospital outcomes and readmission rates for patients with trauma. *Journal of Trauma and Acute Care Surgery, 73*(2), 474-478.	- Care by NP's equivalent to residents - Reduced length of stay.
Gillard, J., Szoke, A., Hoff, W., Wainwright, G., Stehly, C., & Toedter, L. (2011). Utilization of Pas and NPs at a level I trauma center: effects on outcomes. *Journal of the American Academy of Physician Assistants, 24*(7), 40-43.	- NP's/PA's reduced ICU length of stay - No difference in incidence of complications compared to physicians.
Gershengorn, H., Wunsch, H. Wahab, R., Leaf, D., Brodie, D., Li. G., & Factor, P. (2011). Impact of nonphysician staffing on outcomes in a medical ICU. *Chest, 139*(6), 1347-1353.	- No difference in hospital mortality or length of stay compared to physicians
Ohman-Strickland, P.A. et al. (2008). Quality Diabetes Care in Family Medicine Practices: Influence of Nurse Practitioners and Physician Assistants. *Annals of Medicine, 6*, 14-22.	- NP's more likely than MD's or PA's to do hemoglobin A1C, lipid levels, and kidney function testing.
Carter, A. & Chochinov, A. (2007). A systemic review of the impact of nurse practitioners on cost, quality of care, satisfaction, and wait times in the emergency department. *Canadian Journal of Emergency Medicine, 9*(4), 286-295.	- Reduced wait time - Increased access to care - Same quality care as residents
Wilson, I.B. et al. (2005). Quality of HIV care provided by Nurse Practitioners, Physician Assistants, and Physicians. *Annals of Internal Medicine, 143*(10), 729-736.	- NP's provided quality care similar to physician HIV experts and better than non-experts - NP's more likely to do cervical cancer screening than both infectious disease specialists and HIV specialist physicians

Mundiger, I.O. et. Al (2000). Primary care outcomes in patients treated by nurse practitioners or physicians. JAMA, 283(1), 59-68	- Comparable on all outcomes, except NPs did better on diastolic blood pressure control

Nurse Practitioners are cost effective

The cost effectiveness of NP's has been examined and established through research. Many of the articles in table 12-1 illustrate reduction in length of stay, admission or readmission rates, and improved patient outcomes, which are linked to cost savings. A listing of only a few other recent research-based publications on the cost effectiveness of NPs is listed in Table 12-2 below.

NP's are not only frequently paid less, but also deliver primary care in a more cost effective manner than physicians. The cost effectiveness of NP practice was first established with the landmark report of the Congressional Office of Technology Assessment commissioned by the Congressional Budget Office (1979), which concluded that NP's can deliver as much as 80% of the primary care health services, and up to 90% of the pediatric primary care provided by physicians, and do so in an equal or better quality at a lower cost. The American Academy of Nurse Practitioners (AANP) has created a handout documenting the cost effectiveness of NP's (https://www.aanp.org/images/documents/publications/costeffectiveness.pdf) as has the National Nursing Centers Consortium (http://www.nncc.us/site/images/pdf/cost-effectiveness_npcare.pdf). Both are excellent for use in promoting the profession.

Table 12-2: Research and Systematic Reviews on NP Cost Effectiveness

Lancy, S., Zarrabi, M., Martin-Misener, R., Donald, F. … Marshall, D., (2016). Cost-effectiveness of a nurse practitioner-family physician model of care in a nursing home: controlled before and after study. *Journal of Advanced Nursing, 72*(9), 2138-2152.
Martin-Misener, R., Harbman, P., Donald, F., Ried, K., … DiCenso, A. (2015). Cost-effectiveness of nurse practitioners in primary and specialized ambulatory care: systematic review. *BMJ Open, 5*(6). Retrieved from http://bmjopen.bmj.com/content/5/6/e007167.full
Kapu, A., Kleinpell, R., & Pilon, B. (2014). Quality and financial impact of adding nurse practitioners to inpatient care teams. *Journal of Nursing Administration, 44*(2), 87-96
Hauschild, T., Fu, K., Hipwell, R., Baraghoshi, G., Nirula, R., Kimball, E., & Barton, R., (2012). Safe, timely, convenient, and cost-effective: A single-center experience with bedside placement of enteral feeding tubes by midlevel providers using fluoroscopic guidance. *American Journal of Surgery, 204*(6), 958-962.
Blackmore, C., Edwards, J., Searles, C., Wechter, D., Mecklenburg, R. & Kaplan, G. (2013). Nurse practitioner-staffed clinic at Virginia Mason improves care and lowers cost for women with benign breast conditions. *Health Affairs, 32*(1), 20-26.
Schuttelaar, M., Vermeulen, K., & Coenraads, P. (2011). Costs and cost-effectiveness analysis of treatment in children with eczema by nurse practitioners vs. dermatologist: Results of a randomized, controlled trial and a review of international costs. British Journal of Dermatology, 165(3), 600-611.
Dierick-van Daele, A., Steuten, L., Romeijn, A., Derckx, E. & Vrijhoef, H. (2011). Is it economically viable to employ the nurse practitioner in general practice? *Journal of Clinical Nursing, 30*(3-4), 518-529.
Robles, L., Slogoff, M., Ladwig-Scott, E., Zank, D., Larson, M., Aranha, G., & Shoup, M. (2011). The addition of a nurse practitioner to an inpatient surgical team results in improved use of resources. Surgery, 150(4). 711-717.

Nurse Practitioners have high patient and interprofessional satisfaction rates

Many of the studies highlighted also documents high satisfaction ratings with APRN provided care not only from patients but also with professional colleagues. Once patients and physicians are exposed to APRN practice aspects of care such as communication, safety, and satisfaction are often improved (Collins et al., 2014; Goldie et al., 2012; Robinson, Clark & Greer, 2014).

Nurse practitioners have been in existence for many years yet many of us still get the question "What is a nurse practitioner"? Evidence continues to mount that nurse practitioners provide high quality care ranked high in patient satisfaction and cost effectiveness. APRNs receive very little bad press, but also very little press of any sort. The problem with the lack of familiarity with our profession lies solely with us. In order for our profession to be recognized we must promote it. We need to stop hiding behind other professions and organizations and begin to take initiative to advertise our profession and ourselves. Google independent businesses and practices owned by nurse practitioners in your area? How many do you find? The Internet and social media has made NP promotion easy, quick, and affordable. There is no excuse for patients not to be able to easily find you and to have a clear idea of what services you provide.

Step 2: Ensure Recognition

Role Clarification

We must clarify our role in health care to the public, patients, politicians, and health care payers. Consumers need and demand services we are well trained to provide including wellness promotion, illness prevention, personalized education, and empathetic care. We do a great job providing these services now we need to make it known.

Be Visible

When was the last time you were visible within the public, an organization, or your current practice? Make sure that in all professional and community involvement people know who you are and what you do, whether you are a student or a practicing APRN. Make contacts, network, outline your knowledge specialties, and speak up.

Ensure Reimbursement

Reimbursement is crucial for the future of APRNs. The NP role will not survive if there are significant financial barriers. APRNs must seek and ensure inclusion on insurance and managed care panels, and governmental programs at all levels. Each of us should bill directly for our services, rather than through our collaborating physicians so payers recognize us, and our cost effective, quality care. We should also track our own billing, expenses, and revenue generated. Get familiar with the basics of the business of your practice. To be a good steward, you must be knowledgeable.

Full Practice Authority

One of the most recent issues drawing media attention to nurse practitioners is the push in legislation by many states to expand, if not make completely independent, APRN practice regulations. At time of the writing of this chapter, 22 states had independent practice for APRNs (See this interactive map at AANP https://www.aanp.org/legislation-regulation/state-legislation/state-practice-environment). If you state is one of the states with pending legislation or does not currently allow independent practice, know the law, evidence, and facts regarding NP practice and be ready to speak up. This issue can serve as a good conversation starter for expanding public knowledge and recognition on who APRNs are and what we do.

Step 3: Provide Outstanding Patient Care

NP's provide outstanding patient care. We must continue to do so by demanding quality education for upcoming NP's, mentoring, leading, continuing to expand our own individual knowledge, and understanding, interpreting, and actively participating in outcomes based research.

Research is the basis for all evidence and action in healthcare. Without evidence, none of our practice is supported. Professional NP's should be actively engaged in:

- Seeking out current evidence to support daily practice decisions.

- Supporting organizations that fund and disseminate research.

- Ensuring that continued research surrounding NP practice focuses on key areas such as

    o Continued cost effectiveness of NP practice
    o Quality of NP care across cultures and special needs populations
    o Access to care
    o High-level and rigorous research of long-term outcomes of NP care
    o Effectiveness of new nurse and NP led interventions
    o Effects of interprofessional collaboration.

Barriers to promoting the profession

Certainly, we do have a few barriers (good excuses) for the lack of significant promotion of our profession. Have you heard or claimed any of the following as reasons for not promoting APRN practice? What are you doing to overcome these barriers?

Lack of training

Most nurse and NP training is focused on the development of clinical knowledge and skills with very little (if any) business training. Nurse practitioner programs need to continue to focus their attention on the care of the patient, but begin to include business and marketing courses, and at the least specific lessons, to provide business basics to compete in today's health care environment. With the push for continued education through the Doctor of Nursing Practice programs, such courses are now being provided.

Those of us who are no longer in school need to have resources to obtain this information on our own. With the development of Massively Open Online Courses (MOOCs) you can now take beginning business and marketing classes with some of the most prestigious business schools in the country like Harvard or Stanford for free. Likewise, many DNP programs incorporate good financial courses on independent practice.

Costs and Complexity

Marketing and promotion can be expensive. A good ad in the yellow pages can run

$500.00 per month and consider how many people use that product any more.

Newspaper ads may cost the same to run an ad for just one day. Further, the cost and

complexity of online marketing can seem daunting (See this tutorial for help in Google Ad

Words -

https://support.google.com/adwords/answer/6227162?utm_source=help_center&utm_

medium=ha&utm_campaign=education_online_marketing&gclid=Cj0KEQiA6_TBBRDInaPj

hcelt5oBEiQApPeTF6IX-lFbIQOGh3e9fy2_Lp71rYAlXB7CmT6rPakHuzIaAu2x8P8HAQ) and

the use of several social media accounts can be time consuming. Cost and complexity are

barriers to a profession that does not usually make decisions with how monies are spent

within a practice or organization. Chapter 8 discusses some economical marketing

techniques to market both ourselves and thus in return our profession.

Internet marketing and social media provide alternative methods for advertising that

may be more cost effective. For example, development of a blog through platforms such

as WordPress or creating a practice Facebook page is free. To learn more about effective

use of social media as a nurse check out Rob Frasier's (2011) book *The Nurse's Social

Media Advantage*.

Consider also your rating on sites like health grades or Angie's List. Ask patients who

feel they have a good experience with you to go online and fill out a review. Or better yet,

send them a thank you email and link them to such sites.

Controversy in name or nomenclature

An old debate surfaces frequently with regard to our title of nurse practitioner. Many hope for a name change because they believe the title does little to distinguish us from other nurses. Others find interest in a name change that may encompass both nurse practitioners and physician assistants. The debate is fueled many times by the titles of physician extender, non-physician provider and midlevel provider that are frequently used by politicians, physicians, and lawyers. These titles are far from "image enhancers" and are usually used in cases where the person is ignorant about what we do. The AANP has a good position paper on the use of such terms (https://www.aanp.org/images/documents/publications/useofterms.pdf). However, is a name change the answer? Instead of changing our name the real solution to enhancing our image may be "marketing our profession". Only after the role of the NP is clearly defined will the media begin calling NP's for commentary on health care issues.

Time

There is only a set amount of time in each day. Often APRNs take on extra work and responsibilities, leaving little time to promoting the profession. Many very important professional promotion activities take little time. For example, joining a professional organization, staying informed through publications, calling or writing a letter to a state or national politician, or using everyday conversation to expand knowledge on NP practice are quick and effective ways of getting the word out on the importance of NP practice.

The best way to be effective is to schedule some time each week, perhaps an hour, where you work simply on organizational involvement and professional promotion of self and others.

Solutions to Promoting the Profession

    1. Be proactive not reactive

A proactive approach is needed by each and every nurse practitioner. A proactive approach means focusing your attention on the things you can impact, such as the knowledge another person might hold on what a nurse practitioner does. A reactive approach, on the other hand, is focusing on circumstances you have no control over such as the lobbying efforts of another profession. The difficulty lies in knowing which is which.

This is reflected in the Alcoholics Anonymous prayer;

"Lord, give me the courage to change the things which can and ought to be changed, the serenity to accept the things which cannot be changed, and the wisdom to know the difference."

    2. Gain visibility

Tell everyone you have a conversation with that you are a nurse practitioner.

This becomes a daunting task because ultimately it will lead to a needed explanation of what nurse practitioners are and do. However, this is the single best thing we can do to promote the profession. Each person you tell will likely tell others what you told them (or close to it) about our profession. Keep your explanation short, simple, and try to refrain from comparisons or negative talk regarding other health care professionals. Instead, explain our profession as a separate role. At the same time, do not be afraid to use the word "nurse." "Nurse" is a powerful term, which should not impair but enhance our professional image. As previously noted in this chapter, nurses are the most trusted health professional. You may choose to make up your own definition, use those developed by NP organizations, or even use this one if you like:

"A nurse practitioner is a registered nurse with additional graduate training enabling them to diagnose and manage acute and chronic illness, which may include ordering labs, x-rays, other tests, or the prescription of medications. Nurse practitioners tend to focus on the whole person in preventing illness and promoting wellness."

Volunteer to speak at public health events and write articles for public literary sources. Volunteer to do a blog posting for an organization.

Write. The media enjoys having guest editorials and articles written by experts. Nurse practitioners may not be the first choice in expert advice on health related issues, but they will if you make yourself known and available to them (especially on short notice). Start by identifying the reporters in your area who cover health topics for the newspaper, radio, and television. Then make these reporters aware that you are available for quotes on health topics or issues. Many local newspapers and media outlets have public advisory boards frequently looking for volunteers.

3. **Stay connected**

The best way to stay supported, informed, and active is to join a nurse practitioner organization, both national and local. Not only become a member, but also actively engage in local and national meetings. Staying connected means staying both visible and informed. Connectivity brings both visibility and opportunity.

4. Support your peers

We need to make the statement that we prefer to seek the care of nurse practitioners for our own family. Make your decision known to your family, friends, and anyone else you have an opportunity to tell.

Refer friends, family, and patients to other nurse practitioners. Do not be afraid to send a referral to another nurse practitioner that may practice in a setting or specialty other than your own. Speak up for peers, nominate them for awards, and recognize them in conversation with other healthcare providers.

5. Support NP organizations and marketing campaigns

Joining organizations such as those listed in chapter two allow the expansion of the nurse practitioner profession on a national level. Supporting their marketing campaigns means increased visibility to you and your practice and often increased access to quality marketing materials.

6. Advertise

Spend a small amount of your own salary advertising. Build a web site, place a yellow page ad, or even donate to a non-profit agency that will advertise your name and your profession. No matter how small, every effort will progress the recognition of the nurse practitioner profession.

7. Participate in community service

There is not one community without some sort of healthcare need. Perhaps you have knowledge of obesity management, diabetes, or can complete vision screenings for a local health fair. Volunteering within your communities brings visibility to the profession and increases health promotion and health care access in your local community.

8. Learn about politics

Keep a running list of your state and national representatives and the committees they serve on. You must understand the process of how a bill becomes a law to know which legislators to contact and when. Brush up briefly on the legislative process of your state.

9. Have business cards

Business cards are reasonably priced and a quick way to keep your information literally in the hands of others. Whenever you attend a public function or organizational meeting, volunteer, or are out in the community (even on your day off), carry your business cards with you. They are a rapid and cost effective method of keeping you connected.

10. Have an elevator speech

An elevator speech is a quick, clear, and concise method of quickly providing a summary of who you are and what you do. Elevator speeches are never more than two minutes and should be unique to you and your practice or passion as a nurse. You may need more than one elevator speech, depending on audience or project/employment you are promoting, but the bottom line is to know what you want to say ahead of time and practice it. The typical speech includes a statement of who you are and what you do, the problem you or your project/employment solves or offers (an example is good), and a brief list of the benefits. Begin by writing down what you want to say, edit it down, time yourself, and practice. The elevator speech is not meant to be a pressured sales pitch, but a casual presentation of you and your work. This speech goes really well with a business card and is especially good for getting others to back new ideas, projects, research, or programs you wish to initiate. Below are two good business related links on perfecting elevator speeches.

- A quick guide to writing your elevator speech (at Idealist) - http://idealistcareers.org/a-quick-guide-to-writing-your-elevator-pitch-with-examples/
-
- 6 tips for perfecting your elevator speech (at Entrepreneur) - https://www.entrepreneur.com/article/228070

References

Brown, M., & Draye, M. (2003). Experiences of pioneer nurse practitioners in

establishing advanced practice roles. *Journal of Nursing Scholarship, 35*(4), 391-397.

doi:10.1111/j.1547-5069.2003.00391.x

Collins, N., Miller, R., Kapu, A., Martin, R., Morton, M., Forrester, M., ... Wilkinson, L.

(2014). Outcomes of adding acute care nurse practitioners to a level I trauma service

with the

goal of decreased length of stay and improved physician and nursing satisfaction.

Journal of

Trauma and Acute Care Surgery, 76(2). doi:10.1097/ta.0000000000000097

Congressional Budget Office, US Congress (1979). *Physicians Extender: Their Current*

and Future Role in Medical Care Delivery. Washington, DC.: US Governmental Printing

Office.

Ford, L., (1997). A voice from the past: 30 fascinating years as a nurse practitioner.

Clinical *Excellence for Nurse Practitioners, 1*(1), 3-6.

Gallup (2016). Honesty/Ethics in Professions. Retrieved from

http://www.gallup.com/poll/1654/honesty-ethics-professions.aspx

Goldie, C., Prodan-Bhalla, N., & Mackay, M. (2012). Nurse practitioners in postoperative

cardiac surgery: Are they effective? *Canadian Journal of Cardiovascular Nursing, 22*(4),

8-

15. https://www.ncbi.nlm.nih.gov/pubmed/23488361

ICN International Nurse Practitioner/Advanced Practice Nursing Network (2005). Scope of

practice and standards. https://international.aanp.org/Policy/Resources

Kleinpell, R., Scanlon, A., Hibbert, D., Ganz, F., East, L., Fraser, D., Wong, F., & Beauchesne,

M., (2014). Addressing Issues Impacting Advanced Nursing Practice Worldwide" *OJIN:*

The Online Journal of Issues in Nursing, 19(2). Retrieved from

http://www.nursingworld.org/MainMenuCategories/ANAMarketplace/ANAPeriodi

cals/ OJIN/TableofContents/Vol-19-2014/No2-May-2014/Advanced-Nursing-Practice-

Worldwide.html

Newhouse, R., Bass, E., Steinwachs, D., Stanik-Hutt, J., Zangaro, G., Heindel, L, ...

Fountain, L. (2011). Advanced practice nurse outcomes 1990-2008: A systematic

review. *Nursing Economic$, 29*(5), 1-21.

Robinson, J., Clark, S., & Greer, D. (2014). Neurocritical care clinicians' perceptions of

nurse practitioners and physicians assistants in the intensive care unit. *Journal of*

Neruoscience Nursing, 46(2), E3-E7.

Chapter 12

Recent and Relative Reports

We must indeed all hang together, or most assuredly, we shall all hang separately. ---
Benjamin Franklin

Rapid changes in healthcare and practice are best kept up with through continuous

involvement in a professional organization. The purpose of this chapter is to highlight key

reports and trends in practice. Resources for further information on these reports and

trends are provided.

The consensus model for APRN regulation: licensure, accreditation, certification and education (LACE)

The consensus model for APRN practice, otherwise known as the APRN joint dialogue

group report, was completed in July 2008 through the work of both the APRN consensus

work group and the National Council State Boards of Nursing (NCSBN) APRN advisory

committee and endorsed by a multitude of organizations. The report is worthwhile

reading and is available at

https://www.ncsbn.org/Consensus_Model_for_APRN_Regulation_July_2008.pdf.

Current state licensing boards oversee regulations and statutes, but no uniform model

exists for governing advanced practice from state-to-state. In fact, several states meet

very few of the LACE criteria, for example the simple suggestion to use the same acronym for all advanced practice nurses APRN. Florida licenses nurse practitioners as ARNP. Each

state independently determines APRNs legal scope of practice (See the discussion in

chapter 11, with link to full practice authority states at AANP). This discrepancy between

states decreases access to care and uniformity of scope of practice, limiting the ease with

which providers can provide care across jurisdictions and confusing patients who may

seek care in more than one state as to the scope of practice and meaning of the title

APRN. Major points of the Consensus Model include licensure, accreditation, certification

and education.

In the 2010 *Future of Nursing* report released by the Institute of Medicine (IOM)

recommended uniformity in regulations of APRN practice, allowing advanced practice

registered nurses to practice to the full extent of their education. Further, the NCSBN

model Nursing Practice act provides a pathway for each state to build consistent

pathways to practice through licensure. Both point to the importance of LACE.

Because nursing has been a predominantly female enterprise, there are interesting

political dynamics worth analysis. Dr. Nancy Rudner Lugo does an excellent job of

discussing the gender issues in full practice authority and LACE for the ANA publication

the *Online Journal of Issues in Nursing*. Find it here

http://www.nursingworld.org/MainMenuCategories/ANAMarketplace/ANAPeriodicals/OJ

IN/TableofContents/Vol-21-2016/No2-May-2016/Articles-Previous-Topics/Full-Practice-

Authority-for-APRN.html.

Key elements of the model. The Consensus Model centers on seven key elements that

must be uniform across all states:

- Title: Advanced practice registered nurse (APRN)
- Clear definition of the four APRN roles: Certified nurse midwife (CNM), certified nurse practitioner (CNP), clinical nurse specialist (CNS), and certified registered nurse anesthetist (CRNA)
- Dual licensure: as both an APRN and RN
- Graduate education: Required for entry to practice in each role
- Certification: All APRN's to be certified
- Independent practice: APRN's to have the autonomy and authority to practice without physician oversight
- Prescriptive authority: APRN's to have full prescriptive authority without physician oversight (Cahil & Alexander, 2014)

The target date for adoption of these elements was 2015, but barriers remain. In 2009

the NCSBN launched the APRN Campaign for Consensus to assist in adoption of the

model. More information on the campaign can be found at

https://www.ncsbn.org/aprn.htm

Find out where your state stands on LACE, and what you can do with your state ANA and

APRN organizations to help move LACE forward. LACE should be an important part of all

APRN organization strategic legislative plans.

Defining roles of the APRN and specialization. The four roles of the APRN. These four,

CNP, CNM, CNS, and CRNA, are further specified to six population types including, family,

adult gerontology, pediatrics, neonatology, women's health- gender related, and psych-

mental health. Based in the belief that care provided by APRNs should not be limited by a specific setting, but in the needs of the patient, role specialization and recommendations

for additional specialties is to be defined and established by nursing organizations and

special interest groups with the aim of providing specialized practice within each

population described above. For example, the practice of an APRN specializing in primary

or acute care should not be setting specific, but defined by patient and population needs.

Thus newly emerging rolls such as acute care pediatric nurse practitioner are developing.

Recommended regulation of APRN practice at the level of specialization should be

assessed separately from state licensing board regulation. Most importantly, a strong

recommendation is made for APRNs to be independent practitioners without regulatory

requirements for collaboration, direction, or supervision by other healthcare providers.

Core Competencies for Interprofessional Collaborative Practice

Interprofessional education (IPE) is the act of purposeful education where two different

groups of professional healthcare students learn and work together to improve both

collaboration and patient outcomes (Reeves, Perrier, Goldma, Freeth, & Zwarenstein,

2013). In 2009 six different educational organizations, including the American Association

of Colleges of Nursing, joined together to promote IPE and became known as the

Interprofessional Education Collaborative Expert Panel (IPEC). More information on IPEC

can be found at https://ipecollaborative.org/.

As you are likely well aware, a major emphasis has been placed on team-based care.

There have been differences of opinion as to who should lead such teams and/or whether identified leaders are necessary. However, there is little argument on the

interprofessional core competencies needed to ensure effective collaboration and optimal

patient outcomes. In 2011, the IPEC expert panel published Core Competencies for

Interprofessional Collaboration, divided into four domains: values and ethics, roles and

responsibilities, interprofessional communication, and teamwork. The general

competency statements from this publication are included below and more specific

competencies can be found in the report, which is highly recommended reading.

Work with individuals of other professions to maintain a climate of mutual respect and shared values.

Use the knowledge of one's own role and those of other professions to appropriately assess and address the healthcare needs of the patients and populations served.

Communicate with patients, families, communities, and other health professionals in a responsive and responsible manner that supports a team approach to the maintenance of health and the treatment of disease.

Apply relationship-building values and the principles of team dynamics to perform effectively in different team roles to plan and deliver patient-/population-centered care that is safe, timely, efficient, effective, and equitable (Interprofessional Education Collaborative Expert Panel, 2011).

Key concepts included in the report:

Interprofessional education: "When students from two or more professions learn about,

from and with each other to enable effective collaboration and improve health outcomes"

(WHO, 2010).

Interprofessional collaborative practice: "When multiple health workers from different professional backgrounds work together with patients, families, carers [sic], and communities to deliver the highest quality of care" (WHO, 2010).

Interprofessional teamwork: The levels of cooperation, coordination and collaboration characterizing the relationships between professions in delivering patient-centered care.

Interprofessional team-based care: Care delivered by intentionally created, usually relatively small work groups in health care, who are recognized by others as well as by themselves as having a collective identity and shared responsibility for a patient or group of patients, e.g., rapid response team, palliative care team, primary care team, operating room team.

Professional competencies in health care: Integrated enactment of knowledge, skills, and values/attitudes that define the domains of work of a particular health profession applied in specific care contexts.

Interprofessional competencies in health care: Integrated enactment of knowledge, skills, and values/attitudes that define working together across the professions, with other health care workers, and with patients, along with families and communities, as appropriate to improve health outcomes in specific care contexts.

Interprofessional competency domain: A generally identified cluster of more specific interprofessional competencies that are conceptually linked, and serve as theoretical constructs. (Interprofessional Education Collaborative Expert Panel, 2011, p. 2)

The report also contains specific learning objectives, educational tools, learning activities, and defines stages of competency development. In a systematic review, positive patient outcomes of IPE were noted, but more rigorous research is needed to clearly define the impact of IPE (Reeves, Perrier, Goldma, Freeth, & Zwarenstein, 2013).

The Future of Nursing: Leading Change, Advancing Health

The Institute of Medicine (IOM) has also provided support for ARNP practice. The *Future of Nursing: Leading Change, Advancing Health* 2010 publication highlighted four critical messages for the entire healthcare community concerning the role and autonomy of professional nursing within healthcare:

- Nurses should practice to the full extent of their education and training.
- Nurses should achieve higher levels of education and training through an improved education system that promotes seamless academic progression.
- Nurses should be full partners, with physicians and other health care professionals, in redesigning health care in the United States.
- Effective workforce planning and policy making require better data collection and information infrastructure.

The report has implications for all areas of nursing practice, but has had particular impact on APRN practice. An entire review of this document is recommended. The complete report can be downloaded from http://www.iom.edu/Reports/2010/The-future-of-nursing-leading-change-advancing-health.aspx.

Patient Protection and Affordable Care Act (ACA)

The ACA was signed into law on March 23, 2010 by President Barak Obama and represents the most comprehensive overhaul of U.S. healthcare since Medicare and Medicaid were enacted in the 1960's. The goals of this legislation were to increase access and affordability of health insurance while reducing cost of care overall. Some of the key provisions of the law are noted below:

- Insurance must begin to cover preventive services cost free.
- Prohibition of denial of insurance coverage based on pre-existing conditions and rescinding coverage for patients.
- Elimination of life-time limits to insurance coverage and regulation of insurance companies use of revenue
- Requires insurance to spend 80% of their premiums on medical costs.
- Creation of a way for consumers to appeal coverage decisions by insurance companies.
- Creation of consumer assistance programs for navigation of private health care.
- Requirement of insurance companies to cover all applicants within a set of standards and for the same rate to be offered to all applicants regardless of gender or pre-existing conditions.
- In 2011, Medicare began free preventive services and a 50% discount on brand-name medications when they must pay for medications in the 'donut hole'
- Development of accountable care organizations.
- Goal of expanding state Medicaid programs to cover more uninsured individuals
- In 2014, middle and low-income families will be eligible for tax credit to cover insurance costs.
- Shifting in payment for health services to quality and outcomes to increase competition.
- Provision of tax credits to small businesses who provide health insurance.
- Requirement of insurance companies to justify premium increases to consumers. (U.S. Department of Health and Human Services, 2014)

The congressional budget office projects that the ACA will lower future deficits and Medicare spending (Elmendorf, 2013). The American Nurses Association supports this legislation and several key provisions in the law to work to increase the healthcare workforce to meet primary care needs. You can read the legislation in its entirety at

http://www.gpo.gov/fdsys/pkg/PLAW-111publ148/pdf/PLAW-111publ148.pdf

Documentation in practice: HITECH and meaningful use

Title XII of the American Recovery and Reinvestment Act of 2009 ushered in the Health

Information Technology Economic Clinical Health Act (HITECH), which included over 25

billion in government spending to expand health information technology (HIT) and the use

and connection of electronic health records (EHRs) (Centers for Disease Control, 2012).

HITECH set meaningful use standards and financial incentives for health care providers

who convert to EHRs through increased payments by Medicaid and Medicare. Health care

providers and health organizations not utilizing EHRs by 2015 are no subject to Medicare

financial penalties and further roll outs continue as well as exceptions for those that lag

behind.

Goals of meaningful use includes improving quality, safety, efficiency, and reduced

health disparities, improved engagement of patients, care coordination, and population

and public health through the management and access to data, and improved privacy and

security of patient health information (Centers for Disease Control, 2012). However, it

has fallen short on many fronts, and for many reasons. Some include differences in

systems, complexity, companies going out of business after launching products, the drive

for profit over importance, falsification of records by providers charting items that have not truly been done and lack of nurse input. However, benefits of electronically, organized, accessible and researchable patient data are undeniable.

Implementation of Meaningful Use occurs in stages, each with core requirements that providers must implement and prove adherence to. Knowledge of stages and requirements is critical for all providers. The final rule by CMS on Meaningful Use can be accessed at https://www.federalregister.gov/articles/2010/07/28/2010-17207/medicare-and-medicaid-programs-electronic-health-record-incentive-program. Medicare and Medicaid incentives and dates for implementation can be accessed at https://www.cms.gov/Regulations-and-Guidance/Legislation/EHRIncentivePrograms/Basics.html.

Federal Trade Commission: Policy Paper on APRN Competition and Practice

In March of 2014 the Federal Trade Commission (FTC) published a policy paper entitled Competition and the Regulation of Advanced Practice Nurses. The document, based in increasing access to healthcare services through expanding APRN scope of practice, aims to increase competition among health care providers, noting physician supervision requirements a driver of healthcare costs and providing one group of health care providers a market on healthcare.

Key points that legislators and policy makers are called to consider in evaluating APRN practice legislation and restrictions:

- Consumers need access to safe care.
- APRN licensure by states and certification help to ensure safe and effective care.
- APRN's, based on review of the evidence, can safely provide many of the services provided by physicians.
- Competition between providers provides consumer benefits such as quality, reduced cost, and improved access.
- Restriction of competition impacts medically underserved areas.
- APRN's typical collaborate with other providers regardless of requirement.
- APRN scope of practice should have narrow limitations centered only in concerns for safety and not be more restrictive than necessary.
- Safety concerns need to be evaluated for legitimacy.
- Policy changes should be based on current, best evidence and regulations reviewed to ensure that they truly meet the outcomes they are supposed to and do not instead create unneeded restrictions in access to care and competition. (Federal Trade Commission, 2014).

All advanced practice nurses are encouraged to read this important document and to utilize it to help educate legislators and the general public. The report can be found at http://www.ftc.gov/system/files/documents/reports/policy-perspectives-competition-regulation-advanced-practice-nurses/140307aprnpolicypaper.pdf.

Other Reports and White Papers

The focus of this chapter has been on important "do-not-miss" reports that all nurse practitioners should read, but an additional important take-away is that as we continue to progress as a profession, society, and in data and research, that new reports will emerge. Below are a list of other reports that are worth your time in reading. You as an APRN now have the professional responsibility to stay abreast of national, state, and APRN organization white papers and state-of-practice papers.

- NCHE paper on the Current State of Nurse Practitioner Clinical Education-
http://www.aacn.nche.edu/APRN-White-Paper.pdf

-

- NCSB paper on the Nurse's Guide to the Use of Social Media -
https://www.ncsbn.org/Social_Media.pdf

-

- STTI paper on Diversity Resources -
https://www.nursingsociety.org/docs/default-source/position-
papers/diversity_paper.pdf?sfvrsn=4

-

- NONPF paper on the Doctor of Nursing Practice Nurse Practitioner Scholar -
http://c.ymcdn.com/sites/www.nonpf.org/resource/resmgr/docs/ClinicalSchola
rFINAL2016.pdf

-

- The research behind APRN competencies (if you've never read this research
report you should) - http://onlinelibrary.wiley.com/doi/10.1111/wvn.12021/full

-

- Published on OJIN... Addressing Issues that Impact Advanced Nursing Practice
Worldwide
http://www.nursingworld.org/MainMenuCategories/ANAMarketplace/ANAPeri
odicals/OJIN/TableofContents/Vol-19-2014/No2-May-2014/Advanced-Nursing-
Practice-Worldwide.html

-

- AANP practice statements and white papers -
https://www.aanp.org/publications/position-statements-papers

-

- NONPF statements and papers - http://www.nonpf.org/?page=83

References

Cahill, M., & Alexander, M. (2014). The 2014 NCSBN consensus report on APRN

   regulation. *The Journal of Nursing Regulation, 4*(4), 5-12. doi:10.1016/s2155-

8256(15)30111-3

Centers for Disease Control (2012). Meaningful use. Retrieved from

   http://www.cdc.gov/ehrmeaningfuluse/introduction.html

Elmendorf, D. (2013). How have CBO's projections of spending for Medicare and

   Medicaid changed since the August 2012 baseline? In the Congressional Budget Office

blog.

   Retrieved from http://www.cbo.gov/publication/43947

Federal Trade Commission (2014). Policy perspectives: Competition and the regulation of

   advanced practice nurses. Washington, DC: Author. Retrieved from

   http://www.ftc.gov/system/files/documents/reports/policy-perspectives-competition-

   regulation-advanced-practice-nurses/140307aprnpolicypaper.pdf

Interprofessional Education Collaborative Expert Panel. (2011). Core competencies for

   interprofessional collaborative practice: Report of an expert panel. Washington,D.C.:

Interprofessional Education Collaborative. Retrieved from

http://www.aacn.nche.edu/education-resources/ipecreport.pdf

Reeves, S., Perrier, L., Goldman, Jo., Freeth, D., & Zwarenstein, M. (2013).
Interprofessional

education: Effects on professional practice and healthcare outcomes (update).
Cochrane

Database of Systematic Reviews, 2013(3), 1-47. doi:10.1002/14651858.cd002213.pub3

U.S. Department of Health and Human Services (2014). Key features of the affordable

care act by year. In *HHS.gov/Healthcare*. Retrieved from

http://www.hhs.gov/healthcare/facts/timeline/timeline-text.html

Made in the USA
Middletown, DE
04 January 2022

57664178R00120